Unbelievable Crimes Volume Twelve

Unbelievable Crimes, Volume 12

Daniela Airlie

Published by Daniela Airlie, 2024.

UNBELIEVABLE CRIMES VOLUME TWELVE

First edition. August 12, 2024.

Written by Daniela Airlie.

Table of Contents

Introduction

Welcome to number twelve in the *Unbelievable Crimes* series. As always, for those new to the series, let me explain the premise of these anthologies: to explore relatively unknown or lesser-covered true crime stories.

There are no tales of Bundy or Dahmer here; they've been covered time and time again. As barbaric and evil as these men were, believe it or not, there are men and women out there who are just as evil, who have committed atrocities just as disturbing as their spate of crimes. For whatever reason, many of these stories evaded the news and faded into obscurity almost as soon as they were made known.

I can't quite figure out why the likes of Bundy got so much attention, yet many of the criminals I'll cover in this volume got a few local paper headlines before being filed at the back of the true crime vault. Not that I rally for any criminal to get "attention" (it seemed Bundy basked in the infamy he got), but I do feel like many victims never get the remembrance they deserve when the tale of how they died is ignored by the media.

The victims deserve to be remembered and revered and their story told in a respectful way.

On top of that, the criminal ought to be remembered for the vile acts they committed.

While the crimes of Ramirez, Kemper, and Gacy are continuously covered, the crimes of lesser-known criminals are buried. As such, their victims' stories are forgotten. To forget is to allow history to repeat itself.

In this anthology, I cover 20 true crime stories that stood out to me as relatively unknown despite the barbarity and violence of the crimes. From twisted fiends who believe they are vampires to vengeful lovers, Unbelievable Crimes Volume Twelve explores a new batch of case files that have barely been touched over the years.

As I always do, I'd like to offer a quick word of caution about some of the cases in this book. Some are particularly brutal to hear about, including those of sexual assault, torture, or true crimes involving children. With that said, if you're ready, let's begin.

Killing For Infamy

Some cases are so barbaric and sadistic that you find yourself thinking, *surely this didn't happen; it can't be true*. Certain true crime cases are littered with so much depravity and violence we can't quite wrap our heads around the fact that it actually happened.

Perhaps it's our mind protecting us, trying to make us believe that such evil doesn't exist in the world and extreme brutality is only reserved for horror films.

It's a bit like suppressing traumatic memories or reimagining history to convince ourselves things weren't as bad as they actually were at the time. We often refuse to accept the true horrors of certain situations because our mind wants to protect us from facing the upset. Many people behave like this when confronted with true crime stories, too, simply brushing them off as exaggerated for news headlines or fluffed up for tantalizing documentaries.

For some, it may result from a sheltered existence; for others, it's a way to avoid the reality of how harsh the world can be. For true crime followers, we tend to be on the other end of the scale: perhaps overly suspicious, some may say, though all too aware of the dangers of the world.

The case I'm about to cover has provoked reactions of disbelief over the years due to the sheer depravity of the perpetrator. He was as sadistic as you can get, and his one-man crime spree is more like a badly written, gory horror movie than something that happens in real life.

The crimes of Anthony Paul Arkwright were very much real, as was the unimaginable and inhumane torture he inflicted upon his victims. His case is a frustrating one, not just because he evaded capture, which allowed him to target more victims, but because of his sickening motive: he wanted to be famous for his crime spree.

Anthony Arkwright was born in 1967 in Wath-upon-Dearne, a small town in South Yorkshire, England. His childhood was blighted for several reasons; his parents seemingly abandoned him and his five brothers and sisters when they were all very young. As a result, the Arkwright siblings found themselves in the care system.

Care homes in the early 70s weren't considered kind, nurturing places. Back then, it wasn't uncommon for care homes to expose already traumatized children to abuse, either at the hands of staff or the other children housed with them. Some people who endured living in a children's care home at that time have gone on to go on record to speak about their experiences, leaving some to refer to that time as an "epidemic of abuse" in the care system.

It's not clear whether young Anthony was among those who suffered while in care. Still, we do know he exhibited petty criminal behaviors from a young age, and his academic achievements were nonexistent, likely through choice as opposed to inability. As he grew older, his wayward behaviors only escalated, leading him to move from the care system to the youth offending system.

Anthony was plagued by rumors that he was the result of an illegal yet consensual relationship between his biological mother and his biological grandfather. This claim has never been proven, though it's been suggested that Anthony mistakenly thought it to be true.

By the time he was 21, Anthony was a well-known petty criminal, both by the police and members of the small local community. He was someone to avoid; if you saw him walking toward you in the city center, you'd be wise to take a detour to avoid passing him since the young man was senselessly violent, unpredictable, and callous. He would steal without remorse, verbally and physically assault the innocent, and drift in and out of police custody for doing so.

Now, Anthony was over the age of 18, and whenever he found himself incarcerated, it was in an adult prison. He was no wallflower, and his threatening presence likely saw many of the prisoners leave him be as he sat in the prison library, devouring books on serial killers.

As you and I both know, an interest in true crime or serial killers is born from natural human intrigue. For Anthony, though, it was different: it was his obsession. He read killers' biographies as a source of motivation and inspiration. He devoured the story of killer Peter Sutcliffe, the Yorkshire Ripper, as many would enjoy reading their favorite celebrity's autobiography.

His most revered killer was Jack the Ripper. Anthony knew everything there was to know about the unidentified murderer—aside from his identity, naturally—and would mention this to his fellow prisoners, casually telling them that one day, he'd be just as famous as his idol. Even fellow criminals didn't know what to make of the twisted admission; many took it as a macabre joke from an oddball, and others believed that Anthony Arkwright truly was capable of multiple murders. Sadly, the latter would be correct.

Life could have been good for the young man. By the mid-80s, the local council had given him a flat. Factory work and manual labor jobs weren't hard to come by, and Anthony was fit enough to put in the hours and earn a good wage. He could have carved a modest life for himself, perhaps met someone if he decided that's what he wanted, and broken free from his criminal past.

However, he lacked any sort of work ethic. Instead of working or looking for work, he would spend his days indulging in his killer fantasies. Combined with his desire to kill, Anthony also had a passion for survival. There wasn't much to protect yourself from or "survive" in South Yorkshire. The sleepy town was surrounded by fields of docile sheep, and the crime rates in the area were low, aside from the persistent spate of crimes carried out by Anthony himself.

Still, he'd set up camp in fields around the area, surviving the persistent cold weather in a den he built himself. While camping out, despite having a flat to reside in, he'd dream of scenarios in which he'd kill his random victims.

However, state benefits weren't much, and it served Anthony better in finding steady work. That in itself wasn't a problem, but his attitude toward work was. If he got a job, often manual work, he would just not show up or be overtly clear of his disdain toward the job when he did arrive.

In 1988, he was working at a scrapyard, though, as usual, he was careless about keeping the job. His employer had no choice but to let him go after Anthony was absent for several of his scheduled shifts in a row.

Despite not showing any care for the job, Anthony was furious when he was handed his dismissal letter. Along with his termination letter was his final pay, which the incensed man used to go on a day-drinking spree. He downed one pint of beer after another, simmering in rage over how his employer had treated him.

By mid-afternoon, Anthony was staggering and slurring his words. It was at this point he decided to visit his grandfather. When he arrived at his house, the 68-year-old wasn't home, but Anthony knew where he'd be: tending to his vegetables at the allotment. So, the drunken man made his way there and, as expected, saw his grandfather hunched over a vegetable patch. Spotting his grandson, Stanislav Pudoikas greeted him; Anthony reciprocated by stabbing him multiple times.

The force of the flurry of knife attacks paralyzed the victim's spinal cord. Stanislav was still alive but unable to move, blood quickly leaving his body from the multiple knife wounds inflicted by his grandchild.

Anthony then dragged Stanislav into his shed and picked up a heavy hammer. He used this to rain blows to the victim's skull, so much so he crushed it, killing him mercilessly.

The sickening attack was just the beginning of Anthony's spree of depravity. Instead of coming to realize just how horrific and irreversible his actions were, he persisted in indulging his violent fantasies. After years of wanting to emulate Jack the Ripper, it seems Anthony Arkwright had finally decided to act on his urges. More blood spill was to come.

Fueled by exhilaration and alcohol, Anthony resumed his pub crawl. Certainly, he didn't feel any remorse for what he'd done, as was evident by his subtle confession to the barman asking how his day was: "It's been murder on the allotment," Anthony would reply. How could the barman know the patron was being quite literal in his response?

Anthony continued drinking through the night and showed no signs of calming down. People who were also out drinking that night saw the 21-year-old and noticed he was on a high: wild-eyed and acting manically. He would embark on his next terrible crime in the early hours of the next day, August 28.

Former teacher Raymond Ford had long been a victim of Anthony's. For years, the young man bullied, berated, and frequently abused the 45-year-old. Anthony would pick up dog mess and post it through Raymond's door, not in the least bit fearful of being spotted as the culprit. He would smash the man's windows for fun, again unbothered if he'd been spotted carrying out the crime.

On one occasion, Anthony even broke into Raymond's home and stole some of his expensive and sentimental items. Raymond was at a loss as to how to deal with his tormentor's persistent behavior. He decided to report the burglary to the police and told officers that it was likely Anthony who had broken into his home.

This angered Anthony more than usual. His rage came to a head in the early hours of August 28, around 12 hours after he'd mercilessly killed his grandfather.

Anthony returned to his flat after the pubs had kicked him out. Restless and full of murderous intentions, he picked up his devil mask and placed it over his face. His "look" wasn't menacing enough, he felt. He stripped completely naked aside from the mask, left his home, and made his way to Raymond Ford's property. The man's house already had broken windows courtesy of Anthony, which is what the criminal climbed through in order to enter.

Raymond was asleep in his armchair in the living room. Looming over him was a stark naked killer in nothing but a terrifying mask. Anthony, knife in hand, unleashed a flurry of violence on the vulnerable man, stabbing him over 250 times. The knife used, as you expect, wasn't made to inflict such sadistic violence and broke partway through the attack. This didn't stop Anthony from retrieving a new knife and resuming his twisted assault.

This prolonged violence still wasn't enough to quell Anthony's appetite for blood. In a sickening display, he went on to disembowel his victim before scattering his insides throughout his home.

It's been estimated the whole attack lasted about an hour. By this point, it was getting light outside, and Anthony was exhausted from the depravity. Still naked, he returned home, washed the blood from his body, and went to bed.

He awoke just a few hours later. The police were banging on his door, and there was no way for Anthony to escape without them capturing him. He answered the door and was quickly cuffed and taken to the local station. He was frustrated that his spree had to end so soon after it began. After all, Jack the Ripper had killed at least five people.

Anthony's concerns soon evaporated when he realized that the police were only arresting him for breaking into Raymond Ford's house the week prior. They had no clue that Raymond was now dead, lying lifeless in his home in a pool of his own blood. In fact, Anthony was only detained for a short while before being released on bail.

The spree could commence.

After resting for the remainder of the day, Anthony returned to the pub that night. He began drinking heavily again, getting louder and more lairy as the night went on. Perhaps Anthony knew what he was going to do later that night.

In the early hours of August 29, he set his sights on another of his vulnerable neighbors. Marcus Law was just 25 years old and relied on a wheelchair to get around after a motorbike accident rendered him paraplegic when he was younger. Marcus and Anthony were acquaintances, with Marcus often asking Anthony if he could borrow a cigarette. The criminal would often agree, though he would regularly have the favor returned.

Still, Anthony decided that Marcus had taken one too many cigarettes off him over the years. For this indiscretion, he decided, he must die.

Anthony made it to Marcus' home, broke in, and stabbed the man over 70 times. Just like he had with Raymond, the killer tried to disembowel his victim.

Marcus couldn't walk; he stood no chance against his killer.

When Anthony was unable to gut his victim as expected, he picked up one of Marcus' crutches and stomped it straight through his abdomen. Again, the sadism wasn't enough for Anthony. He wanted to defile his victim entirely. He gouged both of Marcus' eyes out and used the sockets as an ashtray.

Anthony then went about his Sunday as usual. By chance, he walked past Marcus' mother in the street later that day and pulled her to one side to offer his condolences about Marcus tragically killing himself. This was news to the shocked mother, who raced to her son's house. What she discovered would haunt her for the rest of her natural life.

The police were called, and Anthony was arrested for the second time in two days.

Once in the interview room with the police, Anthony was arrogant and haughty. He didn't deny anything but gave little in the way of answers. He simply told the police that four people were dead and a madman was on the loose. Four people? The police thought they were dealing with just one victim. Still, Anthony wouldn't elaborate on his comments.

So, the police headed to Raymond Ford's house since he'd most recently complained to them about Anthony's harassment and abuse toward him. The officer on duty, David Winter, never got over the crime scene he walked into. When Raymond didn't answer the door, the concerned officer made his way into the property, following a trail of blood that got bigger and bigger. Then, he stumbled upon an organ on the floor. Looking further, he could see other internal organs scattered on the blood-covered carpet.

Raymond lay in the bedroom. Anthony had said there were four victims; it seems the police had now found two of them, both killed in the same sadistic way.

What about the two unknown victims?

Anthony wouldn't reveal any more than he already had. He spoke in riddles and maintained his conceited attitude toward the police. Almost a week after his arrest, the police found Stanislav Pudoikas lifeless in his allotment shed. Victim number three had been found.

There was just one left.

The discovery of Anthony's grandfather led the police to search the man's property. Inside, they found the lifeless body of 73-year-old Elsa Kronadaite, Stanislav's housekeeper.

Victim number four had been found.

Anthony had no choice but to admit to the killings, except for the murder of Elsa. He denied killing her but did offer strange comments that suggested he was the culprit. Still, there was something else Anthony wanted to confess: he'd killed a fifth person.

The police were now panicking, trying to find the fifth victim before Anthony's trial began. Again, the killer offered little in the way of tangible evidence or leads, leaving the police to blindly search for a body in the local area. When nothing came of it, the police could only surmise that Anthony made up the fifth victim when press coverage of him began to wane. After all, he'd done this with the intention of becoming infamous. Jack the Ripper had five victims at least. Anthony didn't want to fall short of his hero.

When the police let Anthony know they were onto his lies, he began acting out in other ways to stay relevant. In one disgusting display of attention-seeking, he smeared the entirety of his cell with his excrement.

This likely went some way in his trying to convince the prison psychologists that he was insane. After all, no sane individual would act like Anthony Arkwright, would they?

It turns out the comprehensive psychological examinations found that Anthony was incredibly sane. In fact, one of the psychiatrists claimed the killer was "the sanest" of all the people in the prison. A terrifying thought: there is no cure for Anthony Arkwright. He is a cold-blooded killer who knew exactly what he was doing. A sane person committed these crimes.

In the summer of 1989, his trial began. Anthony pleaded not guilty initially, though after some legal counsel, he admitted killing his grandfather, Raymond Ford, and Marcus Law. He maintained his innocence over the murder of Elsa Konradite. The murder of Elsa was ordered to be left on file since there wasn't enough concrete evidence to pin the crime on Anthony.

The following year, he was sentenced to a minimum of 25 years in jail. That meant, by 2015, Anthony Arkwright could be free and walking the streets—he wouldn't even be 50 years old by that point. He most certainly could start life anew after killing four (or more) people with a 25-year sentence.

Then, the UK Home Secretary at the time decided the sentence didn't reflect the seriousness of the crimes. He ordered that he spend the rest of his life behind bars, meaning Anthony Arkwright was handed a whole-life tariff.

There are hundreds of books dedicated to Jack the Ripper. He's been the focus of many documentaries. The sick killer's acts have inspired fictional TV shows and books. Anthony Arkwright, despite his twisted crimes, has simply blended in with every other sick killer in the vault of true crime history. He didn't get the infamy he wanted. We can only speculate if a lifetime behind bars will prompt the killer to feel any remorse or guilt over his crime spree.

For Katie

Revenge is, apparently, best served cold. Curious about the origins of this phrase, I found out it was first coined in the late 1800s and discovered what it really means: that should you want revenge, don't exact it immediately after being wronged. Let the offending party simmer, don't react in the heat of passion, and take your vengeance when the culprit of your pain least expects it. *Let the meal of retribution cool before serving.*

That's what criminal Jared Harris did. However, this chapter isn't about Jared, nor is he the "villain" in this tale. In fact, he's barely a part of the story. He does, however, play an integral part in the ending.

This case began on January 25, 2005, in Crothersville, Indiana. Little Katie Collman had just got back from school. Katie's mom, Angela, was busy in the kitchen making dinner, and her dad, John, was still at work. The small family—including Katie's older sister—lived a simple, happy, working-class life that was bound by their close bond.

Mid-afternoon, Angela realized she was out of toilet paper. Busy in the kitchen, she didn't have time to go to the store. She asked 10-year-old Katie to run a couple of streets over to the convenience store to pick some up. It wasn't far, and Katie had frequently run errands like this for her mother. The girl put on her coat, took the money from Angela, and happily walked to the store.

As she had done numerous times before, Katie picked up the items on her mother's list and took them to the till. There wasn't quite enough change left for any candy, but Katie knew the bank next door had a whole jar of lollipops at the desk, just waiting to be taken. So, toilet roll in her arms, she ventured into the bank, swiped herself a sweet treat, and began her walk back home.

Although Angela was busy in the kitchen, she knew her daughter was taking longer than usual at the store. The area was small, and even if Katie had bumped into a family friend and stopped to chat, it shouldn't have taken her this long to get home. Angela's anxiety soon turned to panic when her husband, John, got home from his shift. She'd been gone far too long by this point. The parents would go looking for Katie but to no avail. There was only a small number of places she would have gone, and there was no sign of her at any of them. The panic-stricken parents called the police, and a missing person's report was filed.

The small town came out in droves to look for the youngster. They were accompanied by the police's search team, who were, in turn, accompanied by cadaver dogs. It was the dogs who picked up on something—Katie's scent by the railway tracks. It seemed to stop there, though.

Then, upon further police inquiry, it seemed Katie had been at the tracks on her way home. She'd spotted a dog lying dead on the railway line, clearly having been hit by a train. She recognized the dog and took it upon herself to knock on the owner's door and tell them the upsetting news. The neighbor seemed to be the last person to have seen Katie before she vanished.

Then, with no evidence to help the police to navigate their investigation, an Amber Alert was issued for Katie. At this time, the police still believed the girl had gotten lost, was perhaps stuck and injured somewhere, or maybe even ran away; they couldn't comprehend that one of their own townsfolk had taken the girl. Much less did they expect her to have been killed since there hadn't been a murder in Crothersville in over two and a half decades.

Word quickly spread around town, and eventually, a witness came forward. They saw a young girl who heavily resembled Katie—mid-length brown hair, petite facial features, wearing a winter coat—in the passenger seat of a truck. The witness also got a good look at the driver, who he described as gaunt, tall-looking, with dark hair and pale skin.

At the time, the witness didn't think much of it since the child didn't look in distress.

Meanwhile, the Collman family were climbing the walls, unable to do anything except wait for the police to find something. Days passed with no new leads, no positive findings, nothing. Then, five days after Katie was last seen, the devastating discovery of her body sent shockwaves through the small community. Katie was found a 20-minute drive from her home in Seymour. Her body had been dumped in a creek, her hands and feet bound. Forensic analysis found that she'd been sexually assaulted prior to her death, which had been caused by drowning.

The Collman family received the news they were dreading. It was worse than anything they'd been expecting.

Then, a man named Chuckie Hickman called the police to offer them a break in the case. He told them he, along with his accomplice Timothy O'Sullivan, had taken Katie from the street and killed her because she accidentally walked into a drug deal. To avoid the girl being a witness to the illegal activity, the pair abducted her, tied her up, and drowned her.

While murder in Crothersville was practically unheard of, so was cracking a case this quickly and easily. At least, the community speculated, it would offer the parents and the rest of the Collman family a small sliver of closure to know Katie's killers would be tried and convicted for her sickening murder. What the community didn't know, however, was that the police were struggling to believe Chuckie's story. He had holes in his confession. Things weren't matching up, and under further police scrutiny, the man's story became downright unbelievable. For reasons unknown, it seemed Chuckie had made the whole thing up.

So, the police focused their attention on the DNA found on Katie's body, as well as the DNA on a discarded cigarette found near the crime scene. It took a few months for the DNA sample to come up with a match, but thankfully, one was found. The

DNA on Katie and the cigarette butt matched that of Anthony Stockelman, a father of three who just so happened to be visiting Crothersville the day the young girl vanished.

He fit the description of the man driving the truck with the young girl beside him; Anthony was tall, skinny, and had dark hair and fair skin. His truck also matched the description the witness gave. This, compounded with the damning DNA evidence, meant there was little room for Anthony to deny his guilt.

So, he didn't deny his guilt. But, he did have an argument as to why he committed the heinous crime: severe emotional disturbance. In his defense, Anthony told the jury at his trial how his father had recently passed away and how this had negatively impacted his mental health.

I imagine you and I have both had loved ones who have passed. When a loved one suffers before their passing, or if the passing is unexpected, this can leave us with all kinds of post-traumatic symptoms. Death is hard; nobody can deny that. Grief can make us do out-of-character things or behave unpleasantly. It can never be used as a reason for or to excuse acts as heinous and sickening as Anthony Stockelman's. The fact that he tried to do so is perhaps a testament to his character.

In the end, the killer was offered a plea deal. To take the death penalty off the table, he would have to plead guilty to murder and molestation. He did so and was handed a life in jail. Naturally, he appealed this. The appeal was rejected.

Maybe some people in the local community wanted Anthony to receive the death penalty. Others perhaps felt this was too quick a way out for him and that a life without liberty was a more suitable punishment. Many others believe that no justice is available for people like Anthony since the punishment can never fit the severity of the crime.

However, unlike a lot of extreme criminals who find themselves behind bars for the rest of their lives, more punishment was to come for Anthony. He was incarcerated with a man named Jared Harris. Jared hated child molesters. He despised killers.

Jared himself was clearly not an angel by any means. He was, after all, behind bars for burglary. But there were some crimes he just couldn't comprehend, and the murder of Katie Collman encompassed them all. More than this, there was another aggravating factor in Jared's rage: Katie was his little cousin.

Anthony was unaware he was living in the same quarters as his victim's family. Perhaps it came as a surprise, then, when one day, Jared, aided by a fellow prisoner, accosted Anthony and pinned him down. Amateur tattooist Jared then took his inking needle out and etched the words "KATIE'S REVENGE" on Anthony's forehead.

Somehow, a picture of the tattoo work was taken and was leaked to the press. The story hit newspapers with the image alongside every article, zoomed in on the red, scabbed-up forehead with shockingly large writing on it.

Jared was tried for battery over the incident. He admitted tattooing the man, saying Anthony agreed to the inking to avoid any future violent attacks aimed toward him. He got seven years added to his 20-year sentence for the infringement.

Anthony remains behind bars, presumably with the tattoo still clear as day on his forehead.

A Sinister Act

In the spring of 1994, Buck and Joy Blodgett welcomed a much-wanted baby girl into the world. They named the little girl Jessie, and from a very young age, Jessie was showing signs of being exceptionally musically talented. It wasn't just making music she was interested in, either; she was a theatrical youngster and adored acting, singing, and dancing, a real theater child in the making. Buck and Joy encouraged Jessie to pursue her passions, and as she grew older, her capabilities and natural talent improved.

As Jessie entered her teens, her empathetic side took over. She'd always adored animals, but when she was able to comprehend the cruelty of the world, she became passionate about animal rights and giving her voice to the voiceless. Her dad would recall the time she ran into speeding traffic to save a turtle who was stuck in the middle of the road or how she only bought items she knew were fair trade. The Blodgetts were justifiably proud of the person their daughter was growing into.

The youngster would become a genuinely kind, compassionate, and decent teenager. That's how everybody who knew Jessie would sum her up.

When she entered her freshman year of high school in Hartford, Wisconsin, she met Daniel Bartelt, another 14-year-old who was also into all things music. The teens clicked almost straight away, bonding over their shared passions. Much like Jessie, Daniel was heavily into acting, although he leaned more towards being the joker of the group. The two would wind up starring alongside each other in some school productions, further solidifying their bond.

Naturally, this transpired in the pair dating at one point, though, as with most high school romances, it didn't last more than a few months. There was no animosity or mean-spiritedness from either person after breaking things off, with Jessie and Daniel coming to the mutual conclusion that they ought to simply be friends. They maintained their friendship right until it came to going to college.

As you'd expect, the intensity of their friendship fizzled out at this time. College offers so many new and exciting experiences and friendships that it can be hard to maintain older relationships, and for a while, Jessie and Daniel lost touch. They'd talk here and there, but nowhere near as much as they used to.

Then, in early 2013, news got back to Jessie that Daniel had dropped out of college and was returning home to Wisconsin. The 19-year-old was elated her old friend was coming back and was excited to make plans to meet up.

In the time that Daniel had been gone, Jessie had done so much with her life. Alongside her education, Jessie opened up her own business to teach kids all things music. It was a success; she had over two dozen regular young clients who wanted to learn to sing or play the piano. Not only that, Jessie's work ethic and infectious way of teaching saw the local church offer a role to direct their choir. Despite still being so young, Jessie had plenty of opportunities for her future.

The same couldn't be said for Daniel Bartelt. Despite his musical talent, he hadn't sought out opportunities like Jessie. He had given college a shot and decided it wasn't for him. Upon his return home in the summer of 2013, he had nothing lined up, and he returned to his parents' house.

Still, the tight-knit friendship resumed, and Jessie and Daniel spent a great deal of time together that summer. The duo bounced off each other creatively and would pen songs together, play instruments, and even record some music together from time to time. Daniel's time with Jessie encouraged him to keep on pursuing his passion for acting, and he got a part in a play that summer. Jessie got her own leading role in a play, too, and the pair were both notably impressive in their respective parts.

On July 14, there was a big wrap party for the cast of Jessie's play. The pool party was documented via photos and videos taken by the theater kids who attended, and some captured Jessie enjoying herself along with her group of friends. Nothing looked untoward, though when Jessie returned home later that night, she told her mother she was upset after receiving unwanted attention from a couple of men who were there.

Jessie told her mother she couldn't understand why the men—who were in their 40s, twice her age—would be interested in pursuing her. On top of that, she was upset that one of the men pulled her onto their lap at one point, something she tried to resist.

In addition to confiding in her mother about the unwanted advances, Jessie wrote about the evening's events in her journal. It was clear that the actions of the two men had bothered the young woman. Perhaps, as is often the case in hindsight, she wished she'd been firmer with the men or been more honest with them when declining their passes. After all, she was known to be kind and polite, and she'd never had to deal with such persistent unwanted attention before. Telling two adult men to knock it off—in a less deferential way, ideally-isn't something Jessie had ever had to do before.

After jotting it down in her journal, she decided she'd get some sleep and would feel better tomorrow.

Joy would check in on her daughter early the following morning, and she saw the teenager was soundly asleep after peeking through her bedroom door. The mother then headed to work and was going to check in with Jessie that afternoon when she returned home for her lunch hour.

When Joy came back home to prepare food and catch up with her daughter, she noticed the house wasn't full of noise as it usually was. Although quiet and mild-mannered, Jessie was loud when it came to her music and singing. The house would often be filled with the sound of rehearsals or Jessie creating a new song, but it was deadly silent. Surely she still wasn't asleep?

"Jessie!" Joy yelled up the stairs, hoping it woke her sleepy teen from her slumber. She yelled again and got no reply from her daughter. Joy took herself upstairs to wake Jessie, and when she entered her room, she was met with a sight no mother should ever have to endure.

Jessie was laid face-up, her skin blue. She had ligature marks around her neck and wrists. Devastation enveloped Joy as she realized her daughter was dead. She called 911, who sent an ambulance, though there was no chance of saving the young woman. Deep down, Joy knew that. By the time she had found her daughter, she was cold to the touch.

Upon finding Jessie dead, Joy noticed something highly unusual. Her daughter's hair and pants were wet as if she'd had a bed bath. Panicked, distraught, and confused, the mother was full of questions that nobody could answer: who did this? Why? And how?

There was no forced entry on the property, no signs of a break-in, and no robbery. The Blodgett family was forced to confront the idea that whoever did this was most likely known to them.

The police who arrived on the scene surmised that Jessie's hair and pants were trying to rid her body of their DNA. A sexual assault test hadn't yet been done, but all the signs were pointing to the fact the young woman had been raped prior to her death. Again, an autopsy had yet to be conducted, but it was likely the cause of death was strangulation via what looked to be a rope.

The Blodgetts were beside themselves. When they questioned how the killer could have gotten to Jessie, they could only think that either Jessie had let them in willingly or they'd known the family well enough to know they rarely locked their door.

I grew up in a small town and know all too well the (perhaps misguided) trust of leaving your doors unlocked. Even on a night, my family would leave the key in the door yet leave it unlocked much of the time. To some, it sounds bizarre, although some communities are genuinely so close that they can live with this type of trust. The fact that my dad also slept with a bat beside his bed suggests this wasn't the case for us, but I digress.

So, the killer was most likely known to the family. They got into the home without much trouble at all. When questioned by the police, Joy immediately pinpointed the two men who were bothering her daughter the night before. She didn't know them, but perhaps they knew enough about Jessie to know where she lived and when she would likely be home alone. Perhaps after being rejected, one or both of them sought revenge?

The police easily tracked the men down since they'd been videoed by other partygoers and were known within the theatrical community. Both men denied having anything to do with Jessie's murder, although they did admit to flirtatious behavior the night before. Nothing inappropriate, they insisted. Though the morning Jessie was killed, one of these men failed to turn up for work. A suspicious coincidence, but nothing to pin him as the killer. Both men were free to go.

Days passed, and the police were at a loss. No leads, nothing.

Let's rewind to a few days before Jessie's murder. In a nearby town, a young woman named Melissa Richards was walking her dog at the local park. It was her usual route, at her usual time, and she'd never feared taking her dog out early in the morning. The park was always peaceful, with other dog walkers here and there.

On this particular summer morning, however, Melissa encountered a malignant young man who approached her with a knife in hand. The man was over 6 feet and was twice her weight. With the addition of the large knife, he naturally struck fear into Melissa. You always think these things happen to someone else, never to you. On this day, it was Melissa's turn to be "someone else." She had three choices, as most victims are faced with: fight back, attempt to flee, or freeze in fear.

Melissa fought.

If she didn't, that would have been understandable: a man twice her size, weapon in hand, stood before her, readying to attack her. There was nobody around to see or hear her screams for help. Still, Melissa chose to fight her attacker before he did whatever he was going to do to her. We often say things like, "Why didn't they fight back?" or "I would have put up more of a fight" when we hear or read about certain crimes. Truth be told, none of us know how we'd react in those situations until we're in them. It's actually uncommon for a would-be victim to fight back as aggressively as Melissa did, though it's lucky she did.

In her adrenaline-fueled state, she grabbed the sharp end of the knife pointed toward her. The blade sliced through her skin, but she held on long enough to show her attacker what he was up against. The two scuffled until the man decided to flee the scene, scared off by his prey's will to survive.

Melissa called the police and told them what had just happened and was able to give a good description of her attacker and the vehicle he sped off in. He was a little over 6 feet tall, wore glasses, and had pale skin and dirty blond, unshorn hair. She estimated his age to be around 20 years old. She said he jumped into a blue minivan, though she was unable to get the license number. She was accurate in where she told the police where he'd been parked, which enabled an officer to recall he'd run that exact car's vehicle plates earlier that day. He'd thought the randomly parked vehicle had looked suspicious enough to want to run a check on it. If he hadn't, then perhaps I'd be writing this chapter as a cold case.

The plates were registered to a couple, neither fitting the attacker's description. However, after questioning the couple, who were in their 40s, the police found out their son, who was at work, was using the car.

Was their son, by any chance, a little over 6 feet tall, did he have dirty blonde hair, and wear glasses? Yes, the concerned parents replied. The police asked for the 19-year-old's phone number to continue their inquiries.

Meanwhile, back in Hartford, Wisconsin, the local community was mourning the loss of a promising young woman. Not only had she been killed, she'd been violated before her death. The Blodgetts were inconsolable. They couldn't grasp how or why this had happened. One of the people who comforted the family was Daniel Bartelt, who had been close to the family for around five years due to his tight-knit relationship with Jessie.

As July was drawing to a close, the Blodgett family arranged a vigil for their daughter. Jessie had done so much in her short time on earth, and it offered her friends and loved ones to reminisce, tell stories about her, and mourn her death together. Naturally, Daniel was in attendance. After all, he was one of Jessie's best friends.

As the vigil was taking place, Daniel's phone rang. It was a short call but an urgent one. He had to leave the vigil immediately. He'd been summoned to the police station. He didn't know why and told those at the vigil he was worried. What did the police want? Surely they didn't think he had something to do with this?

The guests assured the teenager nobody thought he had anything to do with Jessie's awful death and told him the police likely wanted to talk to everyone at some point. So, he duly made his way to the station. Weirdly, he didn't put up much resistance or ask anything about why he was asked to come in for questioning. The police called and requested he speak to them, yet he didn't think to ask why or if he was being accused of any wrongdoing. He simply told them he'd be right over.

Everyone was confident that Daniel had been summoned as part of the routine investigation into Jessie's murder. Nobody thought he had anything to do with it.

They were wrong on both counts.

Daniel hadn't been contacted by the police for Jessie's death, but rather the disturbing attack on Melissa Richards just days prior. When Daniel arrived at the station, he was asked to sit down while the detectives prepared to interview him. The teen complied and was cool, calm, and collected as he chatted away with the station staff. He didn't ask why he was there or seem too concerned at all; this immediately raised a red flag for the detectives preparing to interview him.

"What have you been up to this evening," one of the detectives asked, building a repertoire with the young suspect prior to questioning him. Daniel replied that he'd been at Jessie Blodgett's vigil. She'd been his friend for a few years, he said but had been raped and killed just days before. The detective offered his condolences and began the interview.

It was perhaps a huge shock for Daniel when the questioning wasn't about Jessie but rather the attack on a young woman earlier that month. Daniel denied being at the park that day, though the detective knew the attacker had fought with his victim prior to fleeing the scene. As Melissa told it, they'd fought over the knife, which left her with a nasty wound on her hand. It was likely the attacker suffered a cut or two to his hand, too. Coincidentally, Daniel had a nasty little wound on his thumb, and it looked like it could have been caused by a sharp blade.

The detective questioned the wound, and Daniel brushed it off as a workplace injury. This led to the detective asking Daniel more about his job and what it entailed, which caused him to burst into tears. It was at this point he admitted he'd lied: he didn't have a job at all. He'd been lying about it for months, to everyone. He'd told his parents he had a job to spare them from being ashamed of him. To keep up the ruse, he'd use their car to "drive to work" each morning, though in reality, he just drove around aimlessly.

But this didn't make sense. Why all the tears? And why lie to the police about having a job? What was he covering up; where did he really sustain the hand injury?

Again, Daniel insisted he had nothing to do with the park attack and said he cut himself chopping vegetables. By this point, law enforcement was getting tired of the lies and piled on the pressure. He began talking animatedly, vehemently denying involvement, though detectives weren't buying his protest of innocence. Eventually, when he figured nobody was buying his tall tales, Daniel confessed to being the attacker in the park.

Still, he stressed he was never going to harm the victim; he just wanted to scare her. A macabre prank, as he painted it, was designed to make the lone woman feel full of fear and dread. Even if this were the truth, which officers were sure it wasn't, why would the young man want to do this to someone? To make them feel as scared and helpless as he felt, apparently. Playing the pity card didn't work, though, and the pressure from detectives maintained. In fact, they felt so strongly that Daniel was lying about intending to harm Melissa that they did a thorough search of the park to confirm their suspicions. They thought he may have dropped some incriminating evidence, a weapon he may have stashed for the attack, or a discarded piece of evidence.

They were right. Daniel had tried to hide the tape he intended to use on his victim. It was traced back to the teenager since his blood was found on it. Why would he need tape if his plan was just to "scare" the victim? Tape suggests restraining the woman, which opens up a whole world of sick possibilities for the attacker.

Then, there was a strange passing comment he made prior to the police interview. When asked about Jessie Blodgett, Daniel told the detective that she'd been raped and killed. This wasn't common knowledge. In fact, nothing of the sort had been confirmed. This inadvertent slip of the tongue caused the police to look into Daniel further. They applied for a warrant to search his personal belongings, which was granted. What officers found was beyond anything they could imagine.

Daniel Bartelt was just 19 years old, but his mind was entirely twisted and devoid of appreciation for human life. This was evidenced by what was found on his laptop. There was an untold amount of graphic images and videos, some of which were snuff videos. These gory, disturbing films depicted women being abused horrifically, but one heartbreaking clip stood out among the others. In it, a woman was raped before being strangled to death via a rope. Then, the attacker washed his victim down, just like the killer of Jessie Blodgett had.

When presented with the suggestion that he'd used this horrific video as inspiration for his own murder, Daniel again burst into tears. Frustratingly for detectives, he still denied everything. He insisted he had nothing to do with Jessie's death despite a lot of evidence suggesting he was her killer.

In a unique twist, it seems Daniel's desperation to be believed got the better of him. He was keenly truthful when asked about anything—except the murder of Jessie. So truthful, in fact, he was making himself look more and more guilty. Detectives were getting the teen on their side, getting him to trust that he could tell them anything. In one interview session, he admitted he was writing a book. In it, the main character, Jessica, gets murdered. Another strange coincidence, he asserted.

While Daniel was talking himself into a murder charge, officers were aware they needed solid evidence to make the charge stick.

This is where DNA comes in handy. It can offer irrefutable, bang-to-rights proof that someone is guilty. It seems Daniel believed he'd done a good enough job of washing his DNA from his victim that he'd never be caught.

He was wrong. His DNA was under Jessie's fingernails. He'd thoroughly cleaned other areas of her but neglected her hands. Perhaps his snuff-inspiration didn't include washing the victim's extremities.

The evidence was presented to Daniel. Surely, he'd break down again, but this time, he'd confess his guilt. He did not. He doubled down on his innocence. He was so believable that even Jessie's family doubted the police and their solid dossier of evidence against him. The Daniel they knew would never do that. Sadly, the Daniel they knew wasn't the real one. The real one revealed himself only when alone with vulnerable young women or when alone in front of his laptop.

More damning evidence was to come. A more thorough search of the park where Melissa was attacked found a crumpled cereal box with some disturbing items stuffed inside. A ball gag, some rope, and tape. Forensics tested the items in the box and found both Jessie's and Daniel's DNA on the items. Even without DNA testing the rope, it was clear from the markings on Jessie's neck that the rope was the same one used to strangle her. The bigger portion of the rope, from which the smaller rope was cut, was found in Daniel's room.

A rape test was also carried out on Jessie, which proved she'd been raped prior to her murder.

Now, would Daniel confess? Surely, the police thought, he couldn't keep denying his guilt when there was an abundance of evidence against him.

His trial began in late 2014, and Daniel refused to admit his guilt. Predictably, there was no other result possible than him being found guilty of the rape and murder of Jessie Blodgett. Even after sentencing, Daniel addressed his victim's parents, telling them his conscience was clear, and he prays they hope they find the answers they are looking for. "These shackles don't make me guilty," he said.

If you've ever been a victim of gaslighting or any kind of verbal manipulation, you'll be frustrated at the killer's incessant protests of innocence in the face of irrefutable evidence.

Daniel Bartelt was handed life in jail without the possibility of parole. Naturally, he appealed, though it was rejected.

To imagine a future where someone so cold and callous walks the streets is terrifying. The judge even remarked that the killer would likely strike again, and no doubt his lack of remorse (and refusal to admit his guilt) went a long way in his coming to this conclusion. Life in prison may help Daniel confront any feelings of remorse, guilt, or shame his acts ought to have provoked.

Vampires Do Exist

A vampire is an immortal being or creature that preys upon humans for their blood. Vampires are often depicted in popular culture as mysterious, with superpowers and a mean set of fangs.

John Brennan Crutchley was not immortal, nor did he have long, sharp teeth, though he did stalk and violently attack women to drink their blood.

John was, on the exterior, as far removed from what you expect a real-life vampire to look like. Large, thick glasses took up most of his face while his mid-length fair hair framed what could be described as a rather bookish-looking face. He was slim, unremarkable in his style, and did a good job of simply blending into the crowd. John's abusive childhood may have had a huge impact on his decision, as a young adult, to avoid any kind of attention.

Born on October 1, 1946, in West Virginia, John's entry into the world wasn't met with love and adoration. His parents, William Crutchley and Mildred Burnside, had suffered the loss of their teenage daughter just a year prior to John's birth. The unexpected passing of Donna Crutchley had understandably floored the parents, in particular Mildred. She saw her pregnancy as another chance to bring up a little girl. In some part, she may have believed she was giving birth to Donna again.

There was no disguising Mildred's disappointment when John came into the world. She didn't want a boy, though there was little she could do about it, so she began dressing John in little girl's clothing. Nowadays, there's not too much difference in gendered clothing for children. However, back in the early 50s, little girls wore dresses, which is exactly what John wore up until the age of six at the behest of his mother.

Mildred's resentment towards John spilled into physical abuse. Even William would abuse the boy, with the parents beating him for his childlike infarctions.

As I was growing up, my nana would often say, "Children should be seen and not heard" (in jest, I must add; I believe I made myself very seen and heard as a child). The phrase was commonplace during my nana's childhood in the 1930s, and I believe her upbringing saw her parents take that phrase literally.

By all accounts, the Crutchleys lived by that phrase, too. John practically lived in the basement, rarely interacting with his mother and father as he grew up. He knew better than to bother them since it likely wouldn't end well for the boy. He lived life as quietly as he could, avoiding any attention that may have been bestowed upon him.

As John entered his teens, perhaps to alleviate boredom, he took an interest in fixing electronic items. He'd fix and rebuild radios in the solace of his basement as the other kids audibly giggled and played in the street outside. John never had any friends and became a wallflower at school and at home.

Still, in 1969, just before he graduated with a Bachelor of Science degree in Physics, John met the young woman who would become his wife. The relationship ended as quickly as it began; John had little experience with the opposite sex, and it crumbled entirely when he moved to Indiana. John met another woman whom he quickly married in the mid-70s.

He bounced from job to job, mostly working in electronics for big companies, until he found himself in Florida in 1983, bringing his wife along with him. He got a job at Harris Corporation, a big defense contractor. They were so big, in fact, that they were privy to a lot of information on NASA and spaceborne transmitters for the government, which piqued John's interest massively.

Fast-forward to 1985, two years after John, his wife, and their young child moved to Malabar, Florida.

It was a warm but windy November evening. A young woman had just endured severe bouts of agonizing torture and had managed to escape her captor's clutches. She found herself on the Malabar roadside, crawling to safety as best she could. Traffic sped past her, with truck drivers refusing to stop for the helpless girl. She was beyond disheveled, and her naked body still had cuffs around her wrists and ankles. She was begging for somebody—anybody—to help her.

Vehicles raced by as she cried out for someone to stop. Eventually, a man pulled over, disturbed by the woman's appearance, as she flagged him down. It was clear she'd been through an ordeal. "Don't take me back there," she begged him as she entered the car. The Good Samaritan was clueless as to what she meant. He was going to help her, he promised. The bloodied and distressed woman, who identified herself as Laura Murphy, gave the man details of a house she'd been detained in, repeating that she wouldn't be taken back there.

The man assured her that he was going to get her to safety, after which Laura gave him directions to the house she'd been held captive in. She pleaded with him to remember her directions.

Luckily, the man retained the information Laura gave him. He drove her to his home so he could call the police. 19-year-old Laura was immediately taken to hospital. She had lost a lot of blood, almost half of her blood; in fact, she was at the point where she barely had enough blood left to keep her heart pumping. Had she not been picked up as she crawled along the roadside, she would have surely died.

After being tended to at the hospital, Laura was able to tell her story in greater detail. Even for seasoned police officers, it was disturbing.

She told detectives how she'd been hitchhiking the day previously and was picked up by her soon-to-be attacker. She was heading to Melbourne, Florida, to which the man agreed to take her there. Prior to dropping her off, though, he said he had to return home quickly to pick something up. Once there, he offered the young woman inside his house, which she politely turned down. This, she said, is when the man turned nasty.

He tied something around her neck and strangled her unconscious. She awoke inside his home.

The woman told the police she was laid on a kitchen worktop, with her wrists and feet bound so she could barely move an inch. She looked around the room, searching for something she could use to escape her dire situation. Instead, she saw a video camera and lighting pointing directly at her. It became clear she was going to be the focus of a film she had no desire to be in.

Her attacker then entered the room and violated his victim. Laura told the police that there was videotaped evidence of her rape to back up her story.

After raping her, the attacker inserted needles into Laura's arm and extracted some of her blood. He sipped it right in front of her. "I'm a vampire," the sadist told her before untying her from the worktop. He wasn't about to set her free; instead, he handcuffed her and flung her in his bathtub. Laura remained locked in the bathroom for some time, alone and afraid as to what would become of her. Was he going to drain her of all her blood? Was he doing this alone?

The self-styled vampire returned and assaulted Laura once again in the bathroom. Again, after violating her, he inserted a needle into her arm and drank more of her blood. The young woman was woozy and nauseous, and her energy was quickly depleting from her body. The ability to fight back was quite literally being sucked from her.

Afterward, the attacker cuffed his victim and returned her to the bathtub. He locked the door behind him, leaving her there for the night. She lay alone in the darkness, almost sure she was about to die.

When the man returned the following morning, he repeated his routine: he raped the woman before extracting blood from her. Again, he left afterward and locked the door. Before leaving, he warned her not to try and escape or she'd be killed.

Laura figured it was certain death anyway by simply laying in the bathtub, so she decided she'd make a break for it as soon as she felt the coast was clear. May as well die trying to escape death. The bathroom door was securely locked, so the only way she could escape was through the tiny window above her. She wriggled through it, using the last remaining morsel of energy she could muster. Once she fell to a heap on the ground, she crawled to the nearest roadside, only to be ignored by passing car after passing car.

Eventually, one decent man stopped for her, and now here she was: sitting in the hospital, telling her shocking story to the police after almost losing her life the day before. She was able to offer directions to the property she'd been detained in, as well as a thorough description of her attacker. That same day, officers obtained a warrant to search the home of 39-year-old John Brennan Crutchley.

They entered his home to find him alone. His wife and child were away visiting family for a few days. Officers searched his home and found a tape, just like Laura had told them.

However, it had been erased. They also found a collection of necklaces and locks of women's hair that had been stored away. The police arrested John Crutchley and brought him in for questioning.

While he was in custody, a more thorough search of his home was carried out. Robert Ressler was given the role of spearheading the search team and, after doing so, was open about his opinion that John was most likely a serial killer. During the search, Robert and his team found a stack of index cards with mostly female names etched onto them. There were some male names there, too. Investigators believed there may have been prior victims of the now-named "vampire rapist."

A subsequent search for these individuals saw the police make contact with some of them. They all told an eerily similar story of their interactions with John. Most of their acts had started out as consensual but would quickly turn to nonconsensual when John began to ignore safe words and restrain his victims in sadist ways.

After his arrest, you may presume John's wife was appalled and sickened by what her husband had been up to while she was away. Certainly, she complied with the police and spoke to them willingly. She admitted her husband had certain tastes when it came to intimacy, and when confronted with the rape of Laura Murphy, later brushed it off as "gentle" and noted it was "devoid of brutality."

The search of John's home office also uncovered some disturbing photographs. Some depicted an unidentified woman being choked by him; others were unsettling pictures of women who were unaware they were having their photo taken.

The police, specifically Robert Ressler, felt that they had a serial killer on their hands. Four women had been found dead in Brevard County in the past 12 months, leading authorities to wonder if they'd fallen victim to John Crutchley. They were unable to positively connect him to the killings.

While the investigation was ongoing, John remained behind bars. The evidence against him was mounting, even in a time before sophisticated forensics and DNA testing. His trial began in the summer of 1986, though there was one aspect of his crimes that John refused to admit to: drinking blood.

He insisted that he never drank Laura's blood. This fell under the banner of grievous bodily harm, and John was adamant that this aspect of the charges should be dropped. He admitted extracting the blood but denied drinking it. Tellingly, he told police officers prior to the trial that he'd been introduced to blood drinking by a nurse in the 70s.

If we rewind back in time, from the 70s onward, we can see a clear pattern of death following John as he moved from state to state over the years. The police retraced his steps and noticed a macabre pattern of women winding up dead wherever he went. In 1978, his girlfriend, Deborah Fitzjohn, disappeared.

John was hauled in for questioning at the time but denied knowing where she'd gone. As far as he was concerned, she left his mobile home one day and never returned. Deborah's remains were found in 1979, resulting in a murder investigation taking place. Tellingly, among John's belongings was the business card of the lead investigator of Deborah's murder. Still, there was no definite proof to tie John to her death.

Also among John's personal belongings was the ID of Patti Volansky, a 29-year-old who had disappeared in the spring of 1985. When presented with the finding, John admitted he picked her up when she was hitchhiking but dropped her off before her destination after she became disagreeable. He claimed she dropped her ID in the passenger seat, and he simply stored it in his office. Patti Volansky is still missing.

A further inspection of John's office found he had a stack of female ID cards. Among them was Nancy Brown's card, which belonged to another young woman who had vanished. Her remains had been found in 1984. Then there was 16-year-old Cheryl Windsor, who vanished in the spring of 1984. John also had the ID card of Diana Casey, whose remains were found on Merritt Island in 1984.

John denied knowing these women. What utter macabre misfortune, then, that he would find himself in possession of these young women's ID cards yet have nothing to do with their disappearances or murders.

A search of Route 1 in Malabar was carried out, and the remains of multiple women were found. The bodies of Kimberly Walker, Lynn Desantis, and Carol Molnar were uncovered in quick succession. All these women were found not far from John's family home.

Still, nothing more than the rape of Laura Murphy could be pinned on John. Everything else was circumstantial evidence and sinister coincidence.

However, there was an issue with his trial: Laura didn't want to proceed with pressing charges. This was the 80s, a time when sexual assault cases meant women's sexual history was looked into, and the victims were routinely torn apart on the stand. Understandably, Laura didn't want to have to relive the attack more than she already had, let alone face being called a liar. She'd given her evidence as far as she was concerned: a rape kit and a lie detector test, which she passed with ease.

However, the prosecution needed more. They needed her to follow through with the charges lest her attacker could walk free.

Laura was given counseling after her ordeal, and it was after her counselor warned her that other women would be in danger if she didn't stand up to her rapist that she decided to ensure John Crutchley went to jail.

In 1986, he was found guilty of the brutal and sustained attack on her and was handed 25 years to life in jail. When John's wife left the court, she still couldn't muster any sympathy for her husband's victim. Instead, she told of how confused she was over the fuss and attention the case had brought. Perhaps she, too, was a victim of John Crutchley; certainly, that would make her cold-hearted comments a little easier to understand. Her stance may have changed in years gone by.

Fast forward to the mid-90s, and John was back on the streets. He was sent to Orlando after several states rejected housing him. He was free for less than a day before being hauled back to prison for smoking marijuana. He remained here until August 2003, when he died of self-inflicted asphyxiation. It's believed John didn't intend to kill himself but was restricting oxygen to his brain for personal pleasure.

He has never been found guilty of murder, though seasoned detectives firmly believe he is a serial killer who evaded proper justice his entire life. Some law officials believe his victim tally is over 30 young women.

However, thanks to the bravery of Laura Murphy, John Crutchley spent from 1985 until his death (bar one day of freedom) in jail. Without a doubt, this saved many more women from falling prey to his sadistic ways.

The Rebirth

Rarely does a true crime case come close to summoning the levels of frustration this next case does. If there's ever a true crime tale that embodies the phrase "senseless death," it's this one.

Candace Newmaker was born in November 1989, though her early life was marred by abuse. Her mother, just a teen at the time of having Candace, was a victim of domestic violence at the hands of the child's father. As the youngster grew up, she would try to protect her mother from the abuse, using herself as a shield to stop the mother from enduring yet more beatings.

Candace's parents went on to have two more children together, though the chaotic and toxic atmosphere remained. When the child was just four, she found herself taking on the caregiver role for her little brother and sister; a common theme among children brought up in abusive households.

Authorities soon got involved, however, and took Candace away from the family home for her own safety. She found herself, at just five years old, thrust into the foster system. Although she grew up in a tumultuous household to say the least, it was all the little girl knew, and she missed her mother sorely. She was too young to realize she had been removed for her own good, a feeling compounded after she was passed from foster home to foster home.

As is the case with many children in this scenario, Candace became aggressive and difficult with her caregivers. She couldn't comprehend why any of this was happening, and the only thing she could think of doing was lashing out. She had, after all, only been on the planet for five years. On top of that, those five years had been filled with turmoil and aggression.

In 1996, when Candace was around six or seven, she was adopted by a single woman named Jeane Newmaker. Jeane lived in Durham, North Carolina, in a beautiful, big home. She was a nurse and adored children, and although life hadn't blessed her with a family, she wanted to change that by adopting the young girl.

As with any child in the care system, you can expect they may not have had the best life up until that point. Some children find themselves in care due to their parents dying; others find themselves in care because their parents have abused them. No matter the reason, each child is likely to come with their own set of traumas. After finding out about Candace's past, Jeane felt like she could deal with the little girl's behavioral issues. She fell in love with her as soon as she saw her, and her backstory made her want to bestow that love upon her all the more.

The adjustment didn't go as smoothly as Jeane had anticipated, though. Candace's anger and clear disdain for everything was hard for the new mother. She didn't quite know how to manage it. The girl threw angry fits. She would light matches and try to set fire to things, kill Jeane's goldfish, and scream and screech if the woman tried to reason with her.

Bonding with Candace was proving difficult. Jeane simply wanted the girl to love and trust her, though these things didn't come easy to Candace.

A year passed, though, and things seemed to calm down for the young girl. She enrolled in school, which saw her charm her teachers, make friends, and begin to lower the walls she'd built to protect herself.

Still, a comfortable life filled with routine was something the girl still hadn't quite gotten used to. The temper tantrums were still common, albeit less than before, and Jeane still struggled to manage the meltdowns when they occurred. Plus, the girl would frequently break things when she had a fit of rage, and by the time the child was 10, Jeane was worrying that the behavior would never improve. So, she sought out help.

She'd been to several therapists in the past who would give young Candace medication to "alter" her moods. It's unclear what these medications were, but nothing had apparently worked. At a loss, Jeane was introduced to something called "rebirthing." Apparently, it was a new treatment aimed to mimic the experience of being born. It would allow Jeane and Candace to connect fully, overcoming the attachment disorder the girl allegedly had.

Treatment lasted two weeks and began in April 2000 in Evergreen, Colorado. Jeane spared no expense; it cost her $7,000, but the mother was willing to pay whatever she had to connect with Candace.

Week one passed without a hitch. In fact, Jeane felt reassured by the therapy so far, going as far as to think it was enabling her and the youngster to form a closer bond. The second week was the big one, the treatment that would finally see mother and child connecting: the actual rebirthing.

It was—somewhat—what it sounds like.

The therapy sees the individual simulating the experience of being born: pushing yourself from the "womb," seeing the world for the first time, and being embraced by your loved ones upon your arrival. In this case, Jeane would be embracing Candace, with the child apparently feeling the same vulnerability as she would as if she were a newborn.

Connell Watkins and Julie Ponder were the unlicensed therapists carrying out the treatment. The whole thing was to be captured on video, as a typical birth can often be. It would prove to be a fundamental aspect of this case.

The session began by the therapists wrapping Candace in a flannel sheet, tying it, and asking her to lie down in the fetal position. The little girl did as she was told, after which pillows were piled atop her. Connell guided Candace through the session, telling her to imagine herself as a tiny baby warm in her mother's womb. The pillows on top of her resembled the mother's stomach, which Candace was encouraged to push out of.

Julie Ponder and two other therapy assistants brought in more pillows. They were put on top of Candace, who was already beneath a pile of pillows and wrapped tightly in flannel. Then, the therapists began pushing down on the pillows in order to mimic the tightness of the mother's womb in the final stages of pregnancy. Connell urged Candace to push out, coming head first, though the women pushing on the pillows didn't make it easy. Between them, there was over 600 pounds weighing down on Candace as she was urged to "come out."

The child remained in the makeshift womb.

Connell then, bizarrely, told the child that if she stayed in the womb any longer, her mother would die. Still, Candace didn't emerge from the pillows. After all, three grown women were pushing down on her, and the girl was a slight 10-year-old; she stood no chance. Eventually, Candace was able to say, "I can't do it!"

She was audibly crying, letting the therapists know she couldn't breathe. Still, nobody brought the session to a halt, nor did they pull her from beneath the pillows. "I can't breathe," Candace reiterated. "Somebody is sitting on top of me."

This went on for over an hour. The therapists were simply telling the child to remove herself from the "womb" but were actively stopping her by pushing on her with pillows. The little girl began to feel fearful she was going to suffocate to death and made her fears known to the adults carrying out the session.

"Do you want to be reborn?" Candace was asked. "No," she replied, simply just wanting to be free. "Quitter!" was the response from Julie. Candace said she was going to die, to which the woman replied, "Go ahead."

An agonizing 70 minutes passed. Candace had vomited and excreted underneath the pillows, stuck in her mess, unable to move, barely able to breathe, panicking that she was going to die. No empathy was given when she lost control of her bowels. Connell is heard telling her to stay inside the womb with the vomit and excrement.

It had been a while since Candace had struggled and half an hour since she'd last responded to the therapists. So, they removed the pillows and were met with Candace's blue face. She was dead.

Jeane had been sitting watching the entire thing the whole time in another area. It was only at this point she raced to the room, and the emergency services were called. It was way too late to save the girl.

The therapists, plus Jeane Newmaker, were arrested for negligent child abuse. The whole thing was captured on camera, and the case, as unusual as it was, was open and shut. The trial took place in 2001 and saw Connell and Julie convicted of reckless child abuse resulting in death. Both women received 16 years behind bars.

Jeane Newmaker was found guilty of negligent child abuse and handed four years in jail, suspended.

The two therapists who aided Connell and Julie were given a plea bargain, which saw them each handed 1,000 hours of community service.

In the aftermath of the shocking events, "Candace's Law" was introduced in Colorado and Carolina, which prohibited "rebirthing" practices and has since been implemented in other states.

Someone Has To Die

Motives for murder often fall under these three reasons: jealousy, revenge, and anger.

What can encompass all three of those emotions? Romantic relationships. What romantic relationships are especially explosive and intense and are fueled by immaturity? Teenage relationships.

When we reflect on our youthful relationships, we often cringe at our past behavior. Maybe we said stupid things, behaved irrationally or weren't the best version of ourselves in certain partnerships. We're human: we do and say the wrong thing occasionally, especially when we're in our teens and just figuring out the world and the people in it.

My first relationship saw me smite my parents' rules, stay out late (or not come home at all), and generally go through the "wild" phase many kids go through. It was the same for many of my peers, too, despite many of us now grimacing at our youthful behaviors.

For a group of teens in Virginia in the mid-90s, a jealous love triangle wound up turning into something much, much more sinister. Their youthful envy and immaturity saw the group of young girls carry out the unthinkable: cold-blooded murder.

The murder of 18-year-old Stacey Hanna wasn't quick by any means, either. She was tortured to death by those who tricked her into believing they were her friends.

In the summer of 1997, Stacey Hanna moved from Lynchburg to Richmond, Virginia. It was a fresh start for the teenager, a chance for her to really be herself. She found work in a bagel shop and moved into a townhouse with several other young women, including Kelley Ann Tibbs and Dana Vaughn, with another teenager, Tracy Bitner, often staying over. Tracy was Kelley Ann's on-off love interest, so when they were "off," the group wouldn't see her around the South Belmont Avenue property much. When they were "on," though, Tracy was there often.

Then there were 18-year-olds Domica Winckler and Stephanie Cull, who lived close by and would often visit the group of girls. The gang was as you'd expect a group of closely confined teen girls to be: intense, with a tendency to argue and fall out frequently. However, the girls would make up just as quickly as they quarreled, and there would be calm within the group again, for a short while at least.

Kelley Ann and Tracy's relationship was fiery and full of ups and downs. What Kelley Ann didn't know was that, in the background, Stacey was developing a crush on her. When Kelley Ann and Tracy went on yet another break, Stacey saw this as her chance to make a move on the object of her desires. Kelley Ann seemed to reciprocate her feelings.

The two would enter a causal relationship, though, by all accounts, Stacey desired more than this. The other girls in the friendship group felt as though Stacey was borderline "obsessed" with Kelley, passionately pursuing the relationship.

Stacey knew that her lover was often getting back together with her ex and was fearful they'd end up reuniting once more, thus putting the brakes on her new relationship. So, in a bid to get Kelley Ann to cut ties with Tracy completely, she told a lie: she informed Kelley Ann that her ex was already seeing somebody new.

This fib, told out of desperation, would cost Stacey her life.

Kelley Ann immediately went to her ex to confront her about entering a new relationship. She quickly realized that Stacey hadn't told her the truth, which enraged both Kelley Ann and Tracy. It seems the lie brought the former couple closer together, and they toyed with the idea of getting back together. As you'd expect, this greatly upset Stacey, though she could not do much about it. She had to endure seeing her crush being affectionate with someone else right in front of her.

After this, the group felt like Stacey was becoming troublesome, and felt she was doing her best to get in the way of Kelley Ann and Tracy rekindling things. They thought she was telling more lies to make sure their relationship ended completely. Not only that, since Stacey had moved into the shared house, things had started to go missing; food and personal items belonging to the girls all began vanishing. The group pinned the blame on their newest housemate.

The girls would group together without Stacey and talk about her, not uncommon behavior for teen girls, though this gang of young women did more than simply gossip. Soon, their cruel words turned to violent plans.

Stacey needed to be taught a lesson, they agreed—an "ass-kicking," as they put it. As part of said ass-kicking, the girls also decided to introduce a box cutter into their sadistic plan. The sharp blade suggested more than a beatdown was going to happen.

On the night of July 27, 1997—which was mere weeks after Stacey had first moved to Virginia—she was drinking beers with Kelley Ann, Tracy, Domica, and Stephanie. Although things had been rather tense for Stacey in the days prior, her housemates made her think they wanted to make amends and that they forgave her for lying and meddling. This was a relief for Stacey, who found comfort in her new friendship group. She'd been devastated when she felt them slipping away from her. Plus, the idea that Kelley Ann was upset with her caused Stacey a great amount of anguish, so to be invited for drinks was reassuring to the teen.

Little did she know, it was all part of a ruse. The girl gang knew fine well they wouldn't just be drinking together that night. The group got into Stephanie's car, and she drove them to a desolate area off Cogbill Road, which was a perfect spot for covert drinking if you were underage. It was dark, out of the way, and had a spot for swimming, which was what many a teen did on a heady summer night.

Stephanie parked up, and the girls got out of the car. Everyone except Stacey knew what was about to happen. In unison, Kelley Ann, Tracy, Domica, and Stephanie shouted, "One, two, three, four... I love you," before unleashing a relentless attack on Stacey. She was punched, kicked, elbowed, scratched, and slapped by her so-called friends. It was four against one, and the victim stood no chance against her attackers.

Stacey fell to the floor and cowered in the fetal position, trying to protect herself from the onslaught of punches and kicks. Domica took it one step further by picking up a nearby cinder block and dropping it directly on Stacey's head. The impact of the concrete block fractured the victim's skull and very easily could have killed her.

It didn't kill her; it was just one more painful aspect of the horrifying assault she was being subjected to.

Stacey lay on the floor, begging for mercy as the four girls stood around her, mocking and berating her. As Kelly Ann lunged at her with punches and kicks, she demanded Stacey give her "her heart," a sinister request considering what would come next: the introduction of the box cutter.

Each of the young women took turns to slash and stab at Stacey with the sharp implement, passing the box cutter around as if it were a cigarette they were sharing. After the brutal and callous attack, Stacey was covered in blood. Through the crimson covering her face, her attackers could see their victim's eyes pleading for mercy. Zero mercy was shown. In fact, the girls weren't anywhere close to done with Stacey.

At this point in the attack, despite being badly injured and bleeding heavily, had the girls decided to seek help, Stacey would have survived the torture. She'd have been scarred for life, both emotionally and physically, but she'd have been able to live out the decades of life she still had ahead of her.

The four attackers dragged Stacey's limp body and flung her into the trunk of Stephanie's car. They got in the vehicle and pondered what they ought to do next. Dropping Stacey at the hospital was briefly considered, though it was quickly decided that they would be implicating themselves in the attack by doing so. Instead, they reasoned, they would eliminate her as a witness altogether—by killing her.

The girls spent the next half an hour or so driving aimlessly. Stacey had roused a little in the back and had seemingly come to realize the severity of her situation: bleeding heavily while trapped in the trunk of a car. Panic set in, and she began screaming for help. The four attackers were enraged by Stacey's cries and pulled over to a quiet area to silence her.

Once the car was stationary, Domica volunteered to be the one to open the trunk and quieten their victim. She did so by taking the box cutter and repeatedly stabbing Stacey. After the sickening attack, she coldly closed the trunk and returned to the car. Stephanie drove for a little while longer before the group spotted a quiet area at the end of a logging trail that they could use to dispose of their victim. At this point, they were unsure if she was still alive, considering the amount of violence and stab wounds she'd endured.

Upon opening the trunk, to their amazement, Stacey was still stirring. She was weak and helpless, though no guilt or remorse prompted any of the girls to halt their attack or speak up to help the dying victim. Instead, they turned up their savagery.

They dragged Stacey from the car and tore her clothes from her. She was left in nothing but her underwear on the harsh gravel floor. It had been raining, leaving shallow puddles on the uneven road, and the ground had become thick with mud. The dirt covered Stacey's semi-naked body, somewhat masking the crimson that already covered her. Kelley Ann took Stacey's watch from her wrist before the girls resumed their attack.

Stacey lay on her side and was able to pull her hands toward her head and rest on them as if she were in a sleeping position. The girls then unleashed the box cutter on their victim once more, with Stacey's entire body being desecrated by the bloodthirsty gang. In fact, some wounds were so prolonged and brutal that they ran right from her shoulder to her buttocks. The slashes and stabs totaled over 60 sickening injuries.

Knowing she was mere minutes, if that, away from death, Stacey managed to muster the strength to ask her killers for one final request: to call her mother and tell her she loved her. The desperate, heartbreaking request was met with Tracy slicing Stacey's throat. The brutal motion saw the victim's windpipe cut open.

The four girls left Stacey face down in a filthy puddle. The car journey home saw the teenagers buzzing with glee at the atrocious crime they'd just committed.

Unbeknown to them, they weren't killers. Not yet, anyhow. Stacey was still alive at this point. She was clinging to life, blood pouring from every body part she had. Still, she didn't have the strength to move herself from the puddle she was lying in, and she slowly drowned to death as her killers laughed and joked about what they'd just done to her.

Tracy boasted about how she was the one to end Stacey's life, telling her fellow killers how good it felt to slice her neck open. The entire night, there was one other member of the group, Dana Vaughn, sitting in the car as the murder of Stacey Hanna was carried out. By all accounts, she played no part in the attacks and was allegedly too sick from alcohol to know what had been going on. She was too out of it to stop it, let alone acknowledge it had been happening around her. Once back at the townhouse, the gang quickly filled Dana in on the vile acts they'd carried out that night as she drifted in and out of consciousness in the car.

Still, Dana did nothing with this information. She may have been afraid of her friendship group and of meeting the same fate as Stacey. After all, all Stacey did was tell a fib or two. Her lies were quite easily disproved, and her obsession with Kelley Ann was quite clear. Stacey had only behaved the way she did due to her misguided way of trying to woo her crush; deep down, her attackers knew that. If Dana went to the police and told them what they'd done, there's no telling what the girls would do to her. While it's not the same choice many of us would make, Dana felt she had no alternative but to sit on the macabre information of how Stacey met her cruel end.

Days passed, and the girls resumed life as normal.

They carried on with their days as they normally would, perhaps not expecting Stacey's body to be found any time soon. *The elements may get rid of any evidence of her identity*, they thought. However, just days after her murder, the tortured body of Stacey Hanna was discovered.

The police were called, and the investigation into her murder began. There was no solid proof as to who had carried out the twisted attack, though the word "LIAR" was etched onto the victim's skin. It was clear the murder was personal. With Stacey only living in the area for less than a month before her death, investigators honed into her personal life, which consisted solely of Kelley Ann, Tracy, Domica, Stephanie, and a handful of other young girls who frequented their shared townhouse.

Investigators began following the girls, hoping they were inexperienced enough to leave clues or amateur enough for them to confess while they were being monitored. Days passed with no evidence coming to the surface. Then, they tailed Stephanie Cull as she took her car to the car wash. Investigators intercepted and searched her car before she could get rid of the evidence. Inside, they found Stacey's blood and DNA.

Stephanie, along with Kelley Ann Tibbs, Tracy Bitner, and Domica Winckler, were swiftly arrested. The four were tight-lipped, insisting they knew nothing of Stacey's murder, swearing they had nothing to do with it. However, after some intense questioning, Kelley Ann caved and admitted what had happened. In doing so, she caused every other girl's pleas of innocence to crumble. The truth came out, and even for seasoned police officers, it was disturbing.

Domica, in her admission of guilt, said the killing was "just one of those times." When she was pressed further as to what "one of those times" was, she nonchalantly said, "When somebody had to die."

If you condense it down, Stacey died because of her immature way of handling a crush. She told a stupid lie, which was provably a silly lie, and paid the price with her life. She wasn't just killed; she endured untold pain and suffering before her death. To Domica, though, it was merely "one of those times."

At the quartet's trial, the girls pleaded guilty to murder. Stephanie was handed 20 years in prison since the jury felt she played a lesser part in the crime. Despite admitting she'd doled out attacks on Stacey, it was found she provided more of a "getaway driver" role than a pivotal role in the murder, hence her lighter sentence.

Kelley Ann, Tracy, and Domica got life behind bars.

In a bizarre part of the sentencing hearing, Kelley Ann took to the stand and addressed Stacey's mother. She was teary-eyed and, on the surface, looked remorseful, though her words perhaps suggested otherwise. "I'm extremely sorry for what I've done," she said. "It's not only your loss; it's my loss too," she continued. The attempt at an apology infuriated Stacey's mother, who later said the display of regret was a "joke."

"Why is it her loss?" she questioned.

After serving 18 years of her 20-year sentence, Stephanie Cull was released in 2015. The ball was dropped when her release date fell on the exact date of Stacey's murder, which only added to the Hanna family's pain that one of their daughter's attackers was being released.

If only these girls had simply removed Stacey from their friendship group or ignored her immature way of expressing interest in her crush. Not only would Stacey be alive, but they'd probably all be living free, still young, and have the world at their fingertips. I wonder if that "what if" scenario haunts Stacey Hanna's killers as they spend their lives in jail.

Three Brutes

If you've ever followed the blog I created to run alongside this series, you may know I've covered this crime on there in the past. Way more people read my books than my blog, and I believe this relatively unknown crime deserves to have more eyes on it. So, once more, I pull it from the bottom of the ever-expanding true crime case files and cover it again.

Crimes of a sexual nature are confronting, abhorrent, and hard to read about. I often consider not covering them at all for those reasons, but to avoid covering them would mean the perpetrators' actions could potentially be forgotten. With that said, I'm about to cover a truly horrific case involving some truly barbaric individuals.

There is admittedly little information about this crime, but I've pieced together what details are available to offer a coherent timeline of the event.

The 1995 Okinawa rape incident occurred on September 4 of that year when three US servicemen—Marcus Gill, Rodrico Harp, and Kendrick Ledet—all serving at Camp Hansen in Okinawa, rented a van with the sinister intention of kidnapping a girl. They did just that, and their victim wound up being a 12-year-old Okinawan girl. The trio banded together to plot this sinister kidnapping with one sick intention—to horrifically abuse their young captive.

Once the men had their prey in the back of the van, they taped her eyes shut, sick of looking at her wide, terrified eyes. They tied her by the hands and feet, fully incapacitating the petite girl. Two of the diabolical men raped her, Marcus Gill and Rodrico Harp. The third attacker, Kendrick Ledet, claimed he partook in this vile act but didn't actually carry it out—he merely pretended to rape the girl out of fear of his friends hurting him if he didn't join in.

After multiple beatings and sexual assaults, the trio threw the girl out of the vehicle. She was still in her school uniform. The men couldn't have possibly mistaken her true age—something they'd later try to use in their defense—since she was literally in her sixth-grade uniform when they took her.

While the victim didn't speak the same language as her attackers, so she could not catch their names, she got a good look at them before they taped her eyes closed. They were all African American: she described them as big men with imposing figures. The trio were quickly identified and arrested.

The men were tried in Japan, where the culprits and their families claimed they were being unfairly treated due to their race and nationality. This led to a distinct absence of the three criminals' pictures from Japanese news stories about the abduction and rape. In fact, if you look for any new stories on this crime, you're left with slim pickings from Japanese news outlets.

Still, news of the disgusting crime got out. Some say the event caused a surge of anti-American acts and sentiments in Japan, hence why the Japanese government decided to withhold the details of the accused backgrounds. There were even protests held outside the military base, with tens of thousands of Japanese people condemning the vile acts of the American military on their people.

Former US Navy Admiral Richard Macke made a puzzling quote at the time the crime came to light, which did little to help the situation: "For the price they paid to rent the car (the one the trio used in the crime), they could have had a girl (a sex worker)." What an odd quote, I thought upon reading this: they beat and raped the girl they abducted. Did the Navy Admiral think that, if they paid a sex worker for this, these acts would have been okay? Is he saying their only wrongdoing is where they spend their money that night? We can but wonder.

The Admiral paid for this highly stone-hearted comment. He was dismissed from his role and took an early retirement at a reduced pension rate.

The culprits' trial took place in the spring of 1996. Only Marcus Gill pleaded guilty to raping the girl. Rodrico Harp and Kendrick Ledet denied rape. Still, the weight of evidence against them saw each man handed a jail term. Not as long as you'd think, either: Gill and Harp only got a seven-year sentence, while Ledet got six months less. An undisclosed sum of money was also ordered to be paid to the victim.

Seven years in jail for forever traumatizing a child. For ruining her future trust in others. For taking away her teenagehood. For potentially ruining her life.

All men got "other than honorable" discharge from their roles, which is the worst discharge reserved for the worst violations. The three were all released back to the US, where Rodrico Harp would complain about the conditions he was forced to endure in Japanese prison.

One may then be forced to question oneself: What about what the 12-year-old girl was forced to endure?

Kendrick Ledet died in 2006. Ledet had continuously denied raping the girl. However, his death was a murder-suicide, in which he'd raped a woman before strangling her to death. Afterward, he slit his arms open and bled to death.

It was a truly abhorrent case where the punishment certainly did not fit the crime. With decades passing since the sickening event, I can only hope the girl involved—now a woman—has found peace.

Part of the reason I chose to cover this crime in this volume is that the Okinawa rape incident was back in the news a short while ago. It seems history has repeated itself recently: a US soldier serving in Okinawa kidnapped and raped a young girl in late 2023. Naturally, this provoked a resurgence of the original incident being discussed, understandably noting the clear comparisons. There is little more information on the 2023 case since it's still ongoing. The suspect remains in custody in Japan.

Deep Deception

This next case has been defined as embodying "extreme deception" by the Omaha Police Department in Nebraska. That is an understated way to describe the horrifying spate of crimes carried out by Shanna "Liz" Golyar, all for the sake of wooing a love interest.

The story begins in the autumn of 2012 when Liz swiped through potential matches on a dating website. She connected with a man named Dave Kroupa, and the two immediately hit it off. The pair met up, and their connection only deepened from there. Dave was clear about his stance on the relationship, though, telling Liz that he didn't want anything too heavy or serious. He'd only just split with his long-term partner, Amy Flora, and wasn't emotionally ready to jump back into a relationship.

Dave and Amy had two children and had been together for well over a decade after meeting at work. The pair eventually drifted apart, though stayed on good terms for the sake of their children.

When he met Liz, the first woman he'd spoken to after splitting from Amy, she was a breath of fresh air. They were into the same things, like dogs—which Liz had four of—rock music, and watching movies.

The couple enjoyed hanging out, and Liz seemed to accept it when Dave was adamant about keeping the relationship casual. A couple of months after meeting Liz, Dave was introduced to a woman named Cari Farver when she came into his auto shop as a customer. He was amazed by the woman, whom he referred to as being "out of his league." He asked her out on a date, and Cari agreed.

The date went better than either of them expected. Dave was open with Liz about his desire to see other women; after all he'd been in one relationship for over ten years and didn't want to be tied down. However, when he took Cari out for the first time, Liz was blowing up his phone. Dave advised her he was on a date and couldn't speak to her at that time.

Dave then resumed his date and thought nothing more of it. He and Cari ended up getting on so well that when the night came to an end, the couple weren't ready to part from one another. Dave invited her back to his apartment, and when the pair got there, found Liz waiting.

Liz was visibly upset, crying that she was simply picking up her things. Dave was understandably embarrassed that his date was having to witness this. In the end, he asked Cari if he could see her later once he'd calmed things down with Liz. She agreed and went home.

After Liz's stunt at his apartment, Dave put an end to their relationship then and there. She took her belongings and left.

Dave would reconnect with Cari, apologize for what she witnessed, and explain how he'd broken things off with Liz. The pair resumed dating, though both parties agreed they wanted to keep things casual. Cari would often stay the night at

Dave's place since he lived close to her workplace, meaning the two lovers spent quite a lot of time together at the beginning of November 2012.

On November 12, Cari once again stayed over at her lover's in order to get to work early the following day. Dave left to go to work first and kissed the woman goodbye, telling her he'd see her later. He'd never see her again.

Later that day, Dave got a strange text from Cari asking him if she can move in with him for good. This was odd since Dave had been explicit in his decision not to enter a serious relationship. Plus, he felt Cari was on the same page, too; *why the sudden change of heart*?

He replied that he thought they'd spoken about this and that he wasn't able to offer her the type of commitment she was asking for. The reply was unpleasant. "I don't ever want to see you again, I hate you." Dave was understandably shocked by the reply, which also saw Cari confessing to seeing someone else. That was it, Dave thought; the relationship was over. It was a sad end to a fun courtship, though Dave was puzzled as to how and why Cari turned persona so quickly.

But that wouldn't be the last he'd hear from her. Dave received threatening messages from his former flame, a stark difference from the sweet messages he'd received from her in the previous few weeks.

Only, it wasn't Cari sending the abusive messages. It was Liz Golyar. Why did she have access to Cari's phone? Because she'd killed her and taken on her identity.

As Cari, Liz texted the woman's mother, Nancy, to say she'd left to start a new job in Kansas and wouldn't be back until she'd found somewhere for her and her teenage son to live. Naturally, Cari's mother was shocked by the message, but since it was coming from her number, she believed it to be from her daughter. Still, it was way out of character for the 37-year-old woman to simply leave her 15-year-old son behind. The more Nancy thought about it, the more it bothered her. Eventually, she went to the police to report Cari as missing.

There was little law enforcement could do. "Cari" was still sending messages and keeping in contact. They could not do anything; there was no law against starting a new life in a new state, which is what they believed Cari had done. Maybe she'd met someone new, they thought. Plus, Cari had a history of mental health struggles, and when investigators learned the woman had bipolar disorder, tragically wrote her off as having stopped taking her medication and acting out of character.

Of course, none of this was true. The woman had died a horrible death at the hands of Liz Golyar, who was making sure she hid her crime well—by taking on the identity of the woman she killed.

As time went on, Dave was still receiving nasty messages from Cari. Then, one day, he got a text from his ex, Liz, out of the blue; she, too, was receiving threatening messages and emails from Cari. Liz was afraid the woman would act out on her threats to harm her, and she and Dave sought comfort from one another over the troubling situation. It seems, for whatever reason—jealousy, envy, possessiveness—that Cari was targeting them both equally.

As time passed, with their shared harasser bringing them closer, Dave and Liz soon reignited their love affair. As before, Liz would often stay at Dave's, though often, their phones would ping in unison when they were snuggled in, watching a movie or eating dinner. It would always be another threatening message from Cari. The couple would often receive emails from the woman simultaneously, too.

However, Liz sent them by utilizing an app that allows you to schedule texts for a specific time. She calculated when she'd be with Dave and made sure they were together when the messages arrived.

Still, Dave maintained that he didn't want to rush into an official relationship. He wanted to stick to hanging out and providing company for one another. So, as he'd been clear about from the offset, he would date other people, too. But Liz couldn't let him slip away from her again.

Whenever she felt her love interest's eye wandering, she'd schedule another, more manic, text from Cari in order to bring them closer together. When she felt this wasn't working as well as it once did, she upped the stakes: she carried out a horrific deed to maintain her date's attention. She set fire to her home with her animals inside.

Tragically, the pets wouldn't survive. However, it was all part of Liz's plan: the more trauma "Cari" caused her, the more Dave would lavish her with comfort and attention.

After Liz's house was set ablaze, Dave received another sick message from Cari, admitting to setting the house on fire. She said she hoped Liz and her kid were inside when she lit the fire.

At the time, Dave rushed to be with Liz, consoling her over the loss of her "beloved" animals. As he comforted her, she cried over the horrific way her pets had died. Little did Dave know, she was the one who killed them.

After three years of on and off again dating, Dave still didn't want to settle down with Liz. She was getting restless about his lack of commitment, and he was perhaps not as alarmed by the threats from his former flame, Cari, as he once was. Liz knew she needed to do something drastic to reignite the passion and interest from Dave.

In November 2015, three years after she'd killed Cari, Liz sought her lover's attention by going to the police about Dave's other ex, the mother of his children, Amy Flora. She claimed that she believed the threatening texts from Cari were actually sent by Amy, who had killed her. It seems she was trying to kill two birds with one stone here: abolish herself of all blame in regards to Cari's killing and get Dave's ex out of the picture.

However, her shocking allegations would prove to be the unraveling of Liz and her mountain of lies. The police did speak with Amy, who was understandably taken aback by the questions investigators were asking her and cleared her as a murder suspect right away. They did, however, have another suspect on their radar now: Liz Golyar.

While the police were investigating this odd case, Liz suffered a brutal encounter with Amy. She rang the police in December 2015, begging for help. She was in Big Lake Park, Iowa, and badly injured: Amy had shot her in her leg. According to Liz, she was walking alone around the lake when Amy accosted her and shot her before fleeing. She told the police, to their confusion, that Dave's gun had gone missing just days earlier.

Little did Liz know, but she was merely incriminating herself the more lies she told. It was hard to understand why someone would shoot themselves in the leg just to get someone else in trouble, but it seemed that was exactly what Liz had done. Regardless of not knowing her motive, the police believed she was lying: she'd unintentionally shot herself in the foot by shooting herself in the leg. The only way they were going to get to the bottom of the situation was to let Liz weave her web of lies.

They sensed the woman was conniving enough in her lies to want to frame Amy no matter the cost. So, officers pretended they wanted Liz's help in snaring Amy and asked for more details: the more information or evidence she could give them, the better.

It just so happened that Liz had that to hand: emails she'd received from Amy that detailed how she'd stabbed Cari to death and thrown her body into a garbage bag. In other emails she seemingly also confessed to being the person who shot her in Big Lake Park.

After Liz supplied the police with the emails, she expected them to arrest Amy immediately. When they didn't, she asked them what the holdup was. They told her they needed more concrete evidence: for Amy to reveal not only information that only the killer would be privy to but tangible clues the police could use.

Lo and behold, another flurry of emails from "Amy" were sent to Liz. These ones were especially graphic and described how Amy had stabbed Cari to death in her own car. Police believe that Liz was inadvertently giving them all the clues they needed to piece the murder together... and trace it back to her.

They'd already searched Cari's car when she initially disappeared. They decided to take a second look, this time a more thorough one. They pulled the fabric off the car seats and found the passenger seat had a pool of blood on it. Forensic analysis would confirm it was Cari's blood.

The police had enough evidence to arrest Liz and obtain a warrant to search her home. While she denied having anything to do with the murder in her police interview, physical evidence found at her home suggested otherwise. Among her phone and tablet, they found over 50,000 texts Liz had sent pretending to be Cari. There were over 15,000 emails she'd penned pretending to be the woman. These were sent in just a three-year span; I'm no good at math, but when you work out how many messages the woman was sending each day, you wonder how she had time to do anything else.

There was one especially disturbing piece of evidence: a photo Liz had deleted from her camera roll, but the police recovered. It depicted the body of a woman with a distinctive tattoo on her foot—the exact same tattoo Cari Farver sported.

Despite her protest of innocence, Liz was charged with the murder of Cari in late December 2016, four years after she committed the crime. She was handed life in jail, with the possibility of parole taken from the table.

Cari's body has never been recovered.

The Unicorn Killer

Many times, in crime cases, the killer or criminal can evade the wrath of the law for a long while. Either by luck or meticulous planning, some evil in this world goes unpunished—in this life, at least. For killer Ira Einhorn, he did everything he could to avoid being apprehended for the murder of his ex-girlfriend. He was successful, though the law eventually caught up with him—two decades after he'd slaughtered his ex.

On the surface, Ira was a laid-back hippy. He advocated for peace and was passionate about environmental activism. Still, as we know, when it comes to killers (or anyone nefarious), the surface is often just a mask for what lies beneath. Rarely do they outright expose themselves for the heinous individuals they are.

Under Ira's mask of embracing love and peace was a dark, dangerous man who was capable of terrifying things.

Ira Samuel Einhorn was born in May 1940 in Pennsylvania. We know little about his childhood aside from that his upbringing was middle-class and that his family encouraged young Ira to pursue whatever he wanted in life. Ira's career of choice was to be an English teacher, a dream he realized in 1964 after graduating with a major in English.

As is the English language/arts teacher stereotype, Ira wasn't strict with his pupils. He would talk to his students as if they were his peers. Granted, often, there wasn't much of an age gap between Ira and his students. He had just turned 24, and they were often 18, sometimes older. Although he was the adult in this situation, Ira could get on board with students in ways many of the older teachers likely couldn't. This saw Ira talk to his students about the benefits of cannabis and the wild trips LSD takes you on.

As you can imagine, once word of this got back to the university's administration, his contract wasn't renewed. He was let go in 1965, just a year after he was brought on board.

Still, Ira had other passions aside from teaching to keep him busy. While working as a teacher, he used his evenings and weekends to make a prominent name for himself as an activist. He was vocal about his stance on the establishment, his disdain for war, and, ironically, his anti-violence beliefs. He was a known figure among the hippy community in Philadelphia, and his passionate concerns for the environment endeared him to fellow activists.

There was no denying that Ira was charismatic and full of self-belief. His impassioned speeches and articulate way of communicating his credence were enamoring. Certainly, when he gave himself the nickname "Unicorn," people were more than happy to call him it. He gave himself the moniker since his surname, "Einhorn," translates to English as "Unicorn." One may speculate that he also felt some connection to a unicorn: mysterious and mystical.

Ira was considered a guru among the hippy community he was a much-revered member of. He was wise beyond his years, full of advice and ecological knowledge. So much so he was apparently a major part in founding Earth Day. We now know Earth Day as a collective way for individuals to express their concerns about the well-being of our planet. Back in 1970, when the first Earth Day rally was held in Philadelphia, Ira took credit for organizing the event and being the brains behind the movement.

Ira's involvement in the event has since been disputed. Many of those involved in the creation of the rally have said Ira did nothing to contribute to the event aside from hogging the microphone and refusing to move from the stage when he was requested to do so. In fact, if you look on Earth Day's website you'll find no mention of Ira Einhorn, but rather, Wisconsin Senator Gaylord Nelson is named as the movement's organizer. Still, Ira didn't let the truth get in the way of a good story when he told event goers he was the "master of ceremonies."

It was clear Ira had an inflated sense of self, and this trait spilled over into his romantic life. Despite protesting for peace and being passionately anti-violence, he didn't bring peace or love to any of his girlfriends. He was controlling, hard to please, condescending, and abusive to his lovers. Should a woman dare to reject him—the revered "Unicorn"—he would often turn nasty.

Certainly, this was exhibited when he put one of his ex-girlfriends in hospital after he beat her with an empty glass bottle. She tried to break up with him, to which he replied by bashing her skull with the soda bottle. Another girl was strangled mercilessly by him for daring to upset him.

By the time he was in his early 30s, Ira had left a wave of traumatized women in his wake. When he met Holly Maddux in 1972, there was no way she could know of the devastation and hurt he was capable of, and she fell for his charm and charisma. Holly was just 25 when she met Ira and was known to be as kind-hearted and sweet as she was pretty.

Immediately, Ira knew he wanted to have Holly as his next girlfriend. His love-bombing worked especially quickly, even by his standards: Holly accepted Ira's invitation to move in with him just days after meeting one another. What she believed was a gesture of his strong feelings was, in fact, Ira quickly asserting control over Holly. If she were living with him, he'd know her whereabouts, and she'd be easier to control.

As with most individuals of this nature, Ira exposed his true persona pretty quickly after Holly moved in. He switched from being funny, caring, and listening to what she had to say to being dismissive and blunt. Still, Holly clung to the relationship or, more likely, was unsure how to leave her cruel partner. Eventually, she introduced Ira to her family.

From the offset, they had bad vibes from Ira. He'd managed to get his claws so deep into Holly that he felt no shame or awkwardness about berating her in front of her parents or siblings. In fact, Holly's sister would describe Ira as a "bully" who dominated her once independent sibling.

It didn't take long for Holly to become disillusioned with her boyfriend. He was brutal, abusive, and pig-headed. She also found he didn't abide by the beliefs he preached. He wasn't a peace-seeking man but rather an easily angered brute.

For five years, Holly endured Ira's control and coercion, though, in 1977, she finally felt courageous enough to leave her suppressive partner. She knew she'd have to move far away enough to ensure Ira didn't follow her, so she chose New York City, where the relief of freedom washed over her. The 30-year-old even met a new lover named Saul Lapidus. Finally, things were going right for her.

Despite Ira's poor treatment of Holly, she still felt burdened to call him to officially break off the relationship. Ira didn't take Holly's leaving him with any kind of grace or humility. Those traits just simply didn't exist within him. Instead, he was filled with rage and anger: how dare she leave him.

In her haste upon leaving Ira, Holly left a lot of her personal belongings in his apartment, and Ira used this as a bargaining chip to get her to return to the apartment they once shared. He'd already tried to charm her back into his life, and when he figured it wasn't working this time, he reverted to his default setting: abusive. He told Holly that if she didn't return and collect her things, he'd destroy them. Knowing he'd make good on these threats, Holly reluctantly returned to Philadelphia on September 9, 1977.

Nobody ever saw her alive again.

A few weeks after she was scheduled to pick up her items from Ira's place, Holly's parents contacted the police. They'd not heard from Holly since she'd gone to Philadelphia, even though her mother's birthday had been and gone during that period. Holly kept in touch just about every other day, and it was unusual for her not to call her parents. They were apprehensive that something sinister had happened since they knew of Ira's maltreatment of their daughter.

They'd tried contacting Ira directly, but his phone just rang out as if he was never home.

Philadelphia police would bring Ira in for questioning about Holly's out-of-character disappearance, but he wormed his way out of it using his charm and hippy-like veneer. Surely a man who advocated for peace and violence to stop wasn't capable of anything sinister?

Ira's story was that Holly had left him—she'd told him she was going to the shop and simply never returned. She'd finally left him after years of threatening to do so, he told the police. He acted concerned and feigned care for his former lover, charming the police with his environmentalist guru status. They let him go after questioning. If only Ira had been booked for his numerous assaults on former girlfriends, perhaps he would have been kept in for further interrogation, and his apartment would have been searched.

However, Ira's criminal record was clean, and there seemed to be no history of spousal abuse on his file. He was a free man, completely off the police's radar.

The Maddux family knew Ira better than that. He was a callous man who didn't think twice about throwing his weight around, be it physical or verbal. Frustrated by the police's lack of investigation into him, they paid for a private investigator to tail him and try to find any evidence that he had a part to play in Holly's vanishing.

It didn't take long for the PI to find the incriminating evidence the family sought.

During his investigation of Ira, he made some inquiries to those who had crossed paths with the environmentalist. One of the acquaintances he spoke to was Ira's neighbor, who lived directly below his apartment. The young tenant had some interesting things to say about Ira.

On the night Holly vanished, the neighbor recalled hearing screams and bangs from Ira's apartment. Then, in the following weeks, a dark red liquid began seeping from Ira's floor through the neighbor's ceiling, and the gooey liquid had a horrific stench. So, they called in the landlord, who booked some plumbers to fix the issue. When the workmen arrived, they knocked on Ira's apartment door to seek out the root of the issue. He refused to let them in.

It wasn't quite the discovery of Holly's body, but it was definitely interesting. The PI took the findings to the police, and almost two years after Holly vanished, Ira was rearrested for further questioning. This time, though, the detectives made sure to check Ira's property. The area where the putrid, deep red liquid was dripping from turned out to be his closet in his bedroom.

Further inspection of his closet found a tightly locked trunk inside. The officers who attended the property search braced themselves as they opened it, knowing most likely there was going to be a body inside. They were gripped with fear of not knowing what kind of state they'd find the body in or what disturbing sight they might uncover by opening the trunk.

Once the trunk was prized open, in order to get to the body, officers had to unpack the items surrounding it. Air fresheners littered the box, which had been liberally covered in styrofoam packing. Some scrunched-up newspapers filled the corners of the trunk. Once all these items were removed, the true contents of the chest were made clear: a woman's decomposing body.

It was quickly discovered the body was indeed Holly Maddux. Ira was arrested and, amazingly, still maintained his innocence.

Further forensic analysis of Holly found she died from bludgeoning. Her skull was fractured in multiple places. It seems the incident with Ira's ex-girlfriend, whom he bludgeoned with a glass bottle, was a sinister foreboding of what was to come if he wasn't apprehended.

Although Ira was behind bars, he was still able to maintain his control over various high-profile, well-off people he'd met over the years. One woman, in particular, was so enamored with Ira that she agreed to pay his $40,000 bail. Her name was Barbara

Bronfman, a Canadian socialite who had been drawn in by Ira's charm. Barbara was heavily interested in the paranormal, and Ira feigned a passion for the supernatural to lure her in. She truly believed Ira was innocent and was willing to do anything to help him.

The murder trial was due to begin in 1981, four years after Holly had been murdered. Ira wouldn't show. In fact, he had already fled to Europe as soon as his bail had been posted. He had flitted from Ireland to the UK to Sweden, giving himself numerous aliases to evade capture.

For authorities, it was like looking for a needle in a haystack. The only thing the police could do was to monitor Ira's friends in the US, hoping he'd reveal his true location to them.

They knew Barbara Bronfman was still a prominent part of Ira's life, despite him fleeing the country as soon as she paid for his release. In fact, further investigation showed that Barbara was bankrolling Ira's life in Europe, supporting his travels for years.

It would take until 1988 for Barabra to come to her senses. She wound up reading some damning material about Ira and the murder of Holly Maddux. It seems she'd chosen to believe Ira's version of events instead of checking out the evidence stacked against him. However, when she was confronted with the condemning facts about Holly's brutal death, she cut off all support to Ira. She contacted the police in Philadelphia and told them all she knew.

She told them Ira was living with a woman named Annika Flodin in Sweden. Annika, much like Barbara, was wealthy. It didn't take long for investigators to trace the woman, and when they eventually managed to speak with her, she denied being close to Ira. She said he was simply renting a property from her, nothing more, and she couldn't help further. It felt like a dead end, though the police knew Annika was withholding information. Pretty soon, she dropped off their radar, avoiding all contact and eventually fleeing her home. This made it clear she was in cahoots with Ira.

As the police were doing their best to track the killer down in 1993, it was decided to hold Ira's murder trial despite his absence. He was handed life in jail in absentia. While it showed that the law wasn't giving up on chasing the killer, it was far from what the Maddux family wanted: Ira to be extradited and spend his life in a prison cell.

Years passed, and Ira was skillfully reading capture. The US authorities were working closely with the Swedish police, but there was little in the way of leads. Until, in 1997, when Stockholm police managed to obtain Annika's social security number. A scan of her details on the system showed she'd obtained a French driver's license in 1994, one year after Ira was found guilty of Holly's murder. Interestingly, this led investigators to Annika's full name: Annika Flodin Mallon.

She wasn't hard to find. Her home was a converted windmill in the picturesque commune of Champagne-Mouton, France. When the area was swooped on by the police, they hit a jackpot: inside the windmill was Ira Einhorn, aka Eugene Mallon. He and Annika had married, and the killer had changed his name to Eugene.

However, it wasn't as simple as cuffing the man and hauling him onto a plane to the USA. Extradition laws were a difficult thing to put in place, and Ira made sure to exhaust everything he could think of to slow down the process. While the US and France were hashing out ways to get Ira back to the States, he was allowed to remain free in Champagne-Mouton. Despite being found, identified, and arrested, his life didn't change much at all. However, he was under surveillance by the French authorities since he had a history of simply fleeing when the law got too hot on his tail.

Holly was killed in 1977. Her killer was found guilty of her murder in 1993. He was apprehended in 1997 yet was allowed to remain free. It took until the summer of 2001 for France to agree to extradite Ira back to his home country.

It was news he'd been dreading. Knowing what we do about Ira, he perhaps didn't believe he would ever be extradited and that he'd be able to live the rest of his life in comfort in the warm climates of southwestern France. There was one stipulation to Ira's return to the US, though; he had to be granted another trial.

When Ira heard the news, he responded by cutting his throat. You'd be forgiven for thinking this was a suicide attempt, a way to avoid justice. It seems it was one big ploy to garner attention and sympathy since Ira did not die from his self-inflicted wound. In fact, he wasn't terribly injured from it. Instead, he spoke with the French media and invited a TV crew to come to interview him shortly after he'd harmed himself. You can see the interview online; Ira's bloody gash on his neck is clear, but he's coherent and engaging when being interviewed. Once the cameras stopped rolling, Ira went to the hospital to tend to his wound.

Whatever his desired result from the stunt, nobody knows. It changed nothing; once he was out of hospital, he was cuffed and sent back to the United States. He finally stood trial for a murder he'd committed 25 years earlier.

He was still denying culpability. His claim was outrageous: that the government had killed Holly since she knew too much classified information about paranormal activity. He was the fall guy, he complained, and insisted he never laid a finger on his former girlfriend. Plus, Ira said, he was a "Virgo moon." He was helpful and kind, and his place on this earth was to be of service to others. He was not a killer.

The jury didn't take long to deliberate before the verdict came back: guilty. The district attorney would mock Ira's stance that he wasn't a killer because of astrology. She said he and his Virgo moon "are toast." He was handed life in jail without the possibility of parole.

Ira served 18 years of his sentence before dying of natural causes in 2020. Although he was finally captured, he spent more time running from the law than he did facing justice.

What Happened To Ruth?

Ruth Wilson was just 16 years old when she vanished from her hometown of Betchworth in Surrey, England, in November 1995. The circumstances around her vanishing haven't been explicitly noted as being criminal—nobody has been arrested for her disappearance—but they are interesting, to say the least. Ruth's fate is unknown, but there is enough information here to pique the interest of any amateur sleuth.

She was last seen on a chilly winter night by a taxi driver who dropped her off at a secluded beauty spot that offers stunning views of the Surrey landscape. It was odd that Ruth had asked to be dropped off at Box Hill since it was 4:30 pm in November, the sky was already dark, and it was raining. Still, the taxi driver dropped her off as she asked, although he was concerned for the young girl and watched her in his rearview mirror as he drove away.

She stood atop the hill alone, not moving to meet anyone or walk toward the pub that was a few minutes' walk away. The taxi driver was confused since there was nothing but harsh weather and pitch blackness for the girl as she stood stationary on Box Hill. Eventually, the driver lost sight of his fare and somewhat forgot about her as he continued with his shift.

Unbeknown to him, he would be the last person to see Ruth Wilson alive.

Born in 1979 to parents Ian and Nesta, Ruth was a quiet but happy child. She was close to her mother, though tragedy would strike in 1982 when Ruth was just three years old. Nesta slipped and fell down the stairs, a fall that wound up taking her life. At least, that's what young Ruth was told when she was old enough to start asking questions about where her mother was. In reality, Nesta had taken her own life.

You can understand why Ruth wasn't told the truth about her mother's passing. It's a lot for any child to have to comprehend, not to mention burdening them with the feelings of upset, anger, resentment, abandonment, and heartbreak that would undoubtedly follow. Perhaps her father was just waiting for the right time to tell the truth, which never came.

In 1983, Ian remarried to fellow schoolteacher Karen Bowerman, who would become Ruth's stepmother. Ruth grew up to become a bookish, introverted young girl who enjoyed music and practicing the electric guitar. Although she spent a great deal of time alone and indulged in solo hobbies such as reading, she had a small circle of friends she could rely on.

She was intelligent, though the 16-year-old had faced some struggles with her upcoming A-Levels. Her mock exam results weren't as she'd expected, and she took this hard. In fact, she had a report card she was withholding from her parents as it wasn't as glowing as she'd expected.

In October 1995, Ruth confided in one of her closest friends, Catherine Mair, that she felt uneasy about her mother's death. She felt there was something more sinister than her late parent falling down the stairs." She didn't feel like she could broach he topic with her father or stepmother, so Ruth had taken t upon herself to do some digging. According to Catherine, Ruth took herself off to London to obtain her mother's death certificate. It showed her death as being by suicide.

'd imagine Ruth was full of conflicting emotions. She was just 16, and finding out she'd been lied to for 13 years would have seemed life-altering to her. At that age, it can be hard to look at these situations holistically, and it may have been hard for her o understand why she was (rightly or wrongly) never told the truth.

This was just one month before she would disappear forever. In the month between her obtaining her mother's death certificate and her vanishing, Ruth began acting out. She ran away from home, hid out and friends' houses, and would tell her friends' parents that she didn't want to go home. She never gave a reason as to why she didn't want to return home but claimed she was unhappy there.

When Ruth's friend Catherine told her that she was going to move away to Yorkshire, Ruth was understandably sad that her close, perhaps best, friend was moving hours away. Eventually, Ruth asked Catherine if she could move with her, once she'd gotten settled in her new home. The planned move never happened for Ruth; she would disappear just weeks after Catherine left Surrey.

The weekend before Ruth took a taxi to Box Hill was much like any other for the teenager. She met up with her friends Will and Neil. Ruth and Neil had been in a romantic relationship at some point through school but had decided it was best to remain friends. The trio went out for an expensive meal at an Indian restaurant, and when it came to pay, Ruth insisted she foot the bill. Bear in mind that Ruth worked a few hours a week in a record shop; she didn't have much money at all, and her friends knew this. "It will be something to remember me by," she said as she placed the money on top of the bill.

In hindsight, her comment feels ominous.

The following day, as she did most weekends, Ruth kept busy. She attended Sunday service at church, helped at a youth group afterward, and accepted an invite to have dinner at Will's house later that day. There was nothing untoward or strange about Ruth's demeanor, nor did she give off any vibes she was unhappy. Sure, she was despondent about her home life, but a lot of teens become disillusioned with their parents at this age. Plus, she'd just uncovered the upsetting information about her mother's death, so Ruth's sorrow was understandable.

The next day, Monday, saw Ruth readying herself for sixth form, which is the same as twelfth grade in the US, and planned to catch the school bus with her little sister Jennifer. Ruth dressed in her usual ensemble: a red-knitted jumper and black pants that partially covered her short heeled ankle boots. Over her shoulder was a little blue bag which carried one of her most prized possessions: a personal cassette and a collection of tapes.